D1553667

RICHARD CORNUELLE was an executive vice-president of the National Association of Manufacturers from 1966 to 1969. He is the author of *Reclaiming the American Dream*, and lives in New York City.

# De-Managing America

# De-Managing America
# America
## The Final Revolution

*Richard Cornuelle*

RANDOM HOUSE NEW YORK

*0048447603*

Copyright © 1975 by Richard Cornuelle

All rights reserved under International and Pan-American Copyright Conventions. Published in the United States by Random House, Inc., New York, and simultaneously in Canada by Random House of Canada Limited, Toronto

Library of Congress Cataloging in Publication Data
Cornuelle, Richard C       1927–
    De-Managing America.
    1. Industrial management—United States. 2. Bureaucracy. 3. United States—Social conditions—1960–    I. Title.
HD70.U5C67   658.4′00973   74-29590
ISBN 0-394-46386-2

Manufactured in the United States of America

9 8 7 6 5 4 3 2

First Edition

# Contents

# Part I

# The Unmanageable Society

# 1

# Confessions of a
# Social Engineer

Five years ago I was a card-carrying member of the
establishment. I was an executive vice-president of the National Association of Manufacturers. I lived at the University Club. I had a secretary I called my "girl." I had my
shoes shined every day and counted my change. I voted for
Goldwater in 1960 and for Nixon in 1968.

In 1969 I left. I quit my overpaid job, moved out of my
oversized office, and began, hesitantly, to live another kind
of life.

I wish I could say I left the NAM and the buttoned-
down way of living that went with it for some careful,
conscious reason. But I didn't. I left because I had to.
Something inside me simply went on strike. I had worked
for wages all my life. I had taken orders and given them. I

4

had filled out forms and taken tests and smiled at people I despised. Suddenly I couldn't do it anymore.

So I headed blindly for the sidelines, or I thought I did. But, instead, I rediscovered an America I had known once but somehow forgotten.

I moved out of the high-rent district and began to ride buses and subways because I couldn't afford cabs anymore. And I began to see people in a different way than I had done for a long, long time. I saw them quarreling and loving and haggling and complaining. I saw them sometimes sweet and sometimes outraged. I saw them in laundromats and delicatessens and discount houses. I felt their breath on me in the subway. I realized that I was living in America again for the first time in probably twenty years.

I slowly came to realize that I had been living in another, separate world. I had been in the front office too long. Over the years I had acquired a front-office mentality. I knew America mainly from books. I had seen it only as an executive. I had been to conferences and workshops. I had read plans and designed programs. I had been to countless seminars and served on too many commissions.

Twenty years in the front office had conditioned me to see America as a failure. I was conscious only of plans that didn't work, of programs that backfired, and of the spreading sense of frustration and futility in front-office America. But somehow—and this is what I had forgotten— the country had, at least in some ways, kept working anyway.

I began to see that there are two Americas. There is America as it is perceived abstractly in the front office, and there is the America that really happens. Front-office America has failed massively. But the other America, when it is able to escape the control of the front office, works remarkably well.

I began to see that while we are suffocating in front-office statistics about American life, we know damn little about how America really works and hence how we can make it work better.

I began to sense some invisible hands at work in American society. Young people were learning a lot in spite of the fact that none of our front-office educational plans worked. Millions of people were finding reasonably suitable jobs in spite of the fact that none of our front-office "manpower" programs worked. Many Americans were living longer, healthier lives in spite of the fact that our "health delivery system" was reported to be in a final crisis. In a sense that no one noticed, America was somehow moving constructively in spite of the front office.

I came to believe that front-office policy was elementally wrong-headed. All of us in the front office were social engineers. We were forever trying to bend people as if they were bars of steel. We were unconsciously borrowing methods that are appropriate to building bridges and baking biscuits but which have no useful application to human enterprises.

Good things are happening every day in American society, and, with luck, great things will happen. But the authoritarian methods of the front office aren't working. The power of the front office is a myth. Things do not really get done that way and never have.

I realized that those of us who want to improve society need to express that impulse in an entirely different way.

I came most of all to respect the resilience of a society that had somehow survived all our misguided efforts to

6

improve it. And in the process, I came to believe completely in the indomitability of the human spirit. I feel a powerful force pushing us inexorably toward a good society—the steady urgent pressure of men and women straining to be human, to discover and express all the things they can be. And although I can't prove it, I believe the things straining for fuller expression are good things—warmth, understanding, loving-kindness, creativity, laughter. This is the only solid meaning of "the revolution" we talk about so carelessly at uptown cocktail parties.

I thought when I left the front office that I had given up. But I know now that I hadn't at all. I had only outgrown an illusion.

# 2

# Despair

I have seen the future and it doesn't work.

—Anonymous

When Elliot Richardson left his job as Secretary of Health, Education and Welfare, he gave a kind of farewell address. It was a message of total despair. He said: "There is an increasingly pervasive sense not only of failure, but of futility . . . The legislative process has become a cruel shell game and the service system has become a bureaucratic maze, inefficient, incomprehensible, and inaccessible."

This is not Robert Welch talking or even George Wallace. This is a manicured "liberal" Republican from Boston widely respected for his composure and good sense.

He is talking about the most generously financed welfare agency ever assembled in the history of the world, with 109,000 employees and a luxurious budget of $81 billion. The department, in his informed view, was not working.

*The New York Times* did not consider Richardson's valedictory very newsworthy. It was a little six-inch story buried on page 39. The paper gave much more elaborate treatment, including some pictures, to the news that Yale freshmen had gotten their breakfast in bed on the morning before. And the *Times* news editor was right. Ten years ago Richardson's lament would have been big news, with headlines and weeks of follow-up. But times have changed. What Richardson said was not news. Everyone knows HEW doesn't work.

A few weeks before, George Romney had resigned his job as Secretary of Housing and Urban Development. The efforts of his department to build more houses and make cities livable had, he said, failed massively. The federal presence in housing was, Mr. Romney said, "a 100-billion-dollar mistake." And a larger price must still be paid. Mr. Romney figures that a $17,500 apartment, built under the most recent federal programs will cost the taxpayers between $108,358 and $141,854 over the next forty years.

This sense of the failure of federal programs by the men who manage them was becoming universal. Jeffrey Schiller, the head of the Office of Economic Opportunity's research department—which once fairly bubbled with new schemes to fight poverty—said, "Right now, we're kind of looking around for ideas."

Intellectuals, once almost universally confident that a great society could be federally engineered, were spending their energies documenting the failure of federal programs. Even the Brookings Institution said grudgingly that the Great Society programs, many of which were hatched at Brookings, were "not particularly effective." *

---

* In the fifties, a foundation I worked for had given Brookings some money to

The sense of failure knew no limits. It touched old programs as well as new ones. Social security was widely acknowledged as a failure. Participants could buy equal protection from private companies for much less money. Liberals were saying what a few conservative soreheads had predicted from the beginning: that social security had become in practice simply a way to soak the poor.

Eighteen-year-old Peter W. Doe spent twelve years in school in California and graduated. But he can't read well enough to fill out a job application. He's suing the state for a million dollars.

The post office was in perpetual crisis. Nixon had tried to improve matters by "semiprivatizing" it, an idea set in motion by Democrat Lawrence O'Brien. He had, apparently, only made things worse. Pressure was building in Congress to "governmentalize" the post office again.

Charles Scott, the lawyer who fought and won the famous *Brown v. Board of Education* integration case, recently appeared as a friend of the court in a case seeking separate black school systems. "That's what twenty years of disillusionment can do for you," he told reporter Pamela Hollie.

A professor at the University of California, Dr. Sam Pelzman, concluded that federal drug regulation did more harm than good.

Three University of Pennsylvania criminologists, after a painstaking study of juvenile justice, concluded that our present system didn't work and might be causing more crime than it prevented. Prisons, far from rehabilitating

---

evaluate federal lending programs. A Brookings researcher concluded, after two years of study, that federal lending programs didn't work. Brookings gave us our money back, fired the researcher, and suppressed the report.

offenders, served as crime schools. A federal crime commission, after two years of study concluded that "the failure of major institutions to reduce crime is incontestable." Vengeance and retribution aside, it was better not to imprison the average criminal.

In St. Louis, Pruitt-Igoe, an award-winning public housing project, was being torn down as worse than useless.

According to a University of Chicago professor, D. Gale Johnson, the major farm programs—which are supposed to help farmers by managing the supply of cotton, corn and wheat—don't work. Great pains are taken to discourage farmers from planting on land they wouldn't plant on anyway.

Scholars Judith and Lester Lave have written: "If the goal of the medical-care delivery system is the improvement of health, a great deal of money has been spent with no discernible effect."

OEO economist John Weicher found that the $12 billion of federal urban renewal had made a lot of poor people poorer and a few rich people richer.

Peter Bauer, a professor at the London School of Economics, concludes after years of study that foreign aid retards the progress of the countries we send it to.

The sense of failure reached all American institutions, and the agenda of urgent public business continued to swell.

The air is getting dangerously poisonous.

The cities are collapsing.

The police can't keep the peace.

Business can no longer produce things that work.

The health delivery system is not delivering health.

We are running out of fuel.

The trains don't run on time.

Our money is rapidly losing its value at the same time the economy is dangerously slowing down. Most of the people believe we are heading for another Great Depression.

The cities are spending more money than ever before with less effect. And some of them are going broke. Newark's business administrator, Cornelius Bodine, said, "We've sent the state our death notice."

There is thus a tide of disenchantment with practically all American institutions. Louis Harris checked public sentiment on the matter in 1966 and again in 1972. The result was frightening. In 1966, for example, a modest enough 42 percent of the people expressed "a great deal of confidence" in Congressional leadership. In 1972 the figure was a sorry 21 percent. But no other institution scored much better:

|  | *1966* | *1972* |
|---|---|---|
| Medicine | 72% | 48% |
| Finance | 67 | 39 |
| Science | 56 | 37 |
| Military | 62 | 35 |
| Education | 61 | 33 |
| Psychiatry | 51 | 31 |
| Religion | 41 | 30 |
| Retail business | 48 | 28 |
| U.S. Supreme Court | 51 | 28 |
| U.S. Executive Branch | 41 | 27 |
| Major U.S. companies | 55 | 27 |
| Congress | 42 | 19 |
| The press | 29 | 18 |
| Television | 25 | 17 |

| | | |
|---|---|---|
| Labor | 22 | 15 |
| Advertising | 21 | 12 |

The Gallup organization confirmed this sad result. They asked people to rate federal, state and local governments in terms of justice, efficiency and responsiveness. The system, reported *Time* magazine, flunked in all three categories.

The message was clear. For good reasons, practically all Americans were losing confidence in practically all their institutions. There was, in other words, a nearly universal consensus that front-office America had failed.

The question is why.

# 3

# The Obsolescence of Authority

Do you know what amazes me more than anything else? The impotence of force to organize anything.
—Napoleon Bonaparte

The problem is this: authority isn't working the way it once did.

We have traditionally relied on authority, in one form or another, as the basis for our marriages, for rearing our children, for teaching them, for organizing our work, for running our railroads, and, particularly, for the conduct of the public business.

Authority has taken its strength sometimes from plain naked power, more often simply from tradition and convention. But most of our institutions are essentially authoritarian. Marriage has been based on the authority of the male partner. Families are built around the idea of parental authority. Schools are kept in order by the authority of the teacher. Businesses are built around the final authority of the boss. "The worst thing that can happen," says Phillips

14

Petroleum Corporation president William Martin, "is to have an employee that doesn't fit. A corporation has to have regimentation in order to run."

*this attitude is wrong*

When we form a committee to bring culture to Kalamazoo, we first appoint a chairman, and thereafter accept his authority. We can imagine replacing him, but it is much harder to imagine getting along without him.

We have been, for better or for worse, an authoritarian society. And now, suddenly, it isn't working anymore.

Authority is built on subordination. People must be willing to accept subordinate roles, limiting definitions of themselves. And Americans everywhere are becoming insubordinate, unmanageable.

Millions of women are rejecting subordination in marriage. Marriages based on male authority—on the promise to "love, honor and obey"—are simply coming apart. Tracer's Company, a firm which searches for runaways, says that in 1963 it was asked to trace one runaway wife for every three hundred runaway husbands. By last year the ratio had plummeted to one to two. Tracer's president, Ed Goldfuder, says, "Women's lib gives runaway wives the heart to do it."

Children are becoming insubordinate. Parents didn't need Rudolf Dreikurs, the popular child-rearing coach, to tell them: "You can no longer 'make' a child do anything for very long. Force simply does not work." And thus the family, the basic unit in our society, seems to be disintegrating.

The 1970 National Fertility Study conducted by Princeton's Office of Population Research showed that 68 percent of Catholic women had rejected the Pope's clear instruction to rely on rhythm for birth control. Among younger women the percentage was 78 percent.

The Army defines discipline as "a state of mind which leads to a willingness to obey an order no matter how unpleasant or dangerous the task to be performed." But this necessary state of mind is disappearing. Insubordination has become commonplace. A soldier serving in Vietnam wrote in *The New York Times*: "I almost always wear a pair of Keds, a blue tie-dye shirt and army pants I made into cutoffs. I put in an appearance at work sometimes to see if I've gotten any mail." Officers who got pushy were "fragged" in the night—murdered by grenades rolled under their tent flaps.

We lost that senseless war, not because the best and the brightest suddenly saw the light, but because most of our soldiers wouldn't fight it. National policy was effectively made by buck privates in the jungle.

Even the idea of fashion is becoming unfashionable. Designer Bill Blass says:

You can't impose fashion on masses of women anymore. . . . Last year, the designers, the press, the whole industry made it seem the midi was the only choice. So the women hated it. I think women are saying that they don't want to be dictated to anymore.

*W*, the fashion industry's popular weekly, put it more simply: "Nobody can tell women what to wear anymore."

Sociologist Herbert Gans writes: "People . . . are less willing . . . to be bossed around by superiors or by antiquated and arbitrary rules."

Eli Ginzberg, one of our most careful observers of human organization, believes the foundations of Western society are being transformed. "A hurricane is blowing," he writes, and the eye of the hurricane is "the unwillingness of many individuals to accept the authority of established institutions to prescribe their goals and behavior."

. The state of mind necessary to authoritarian management is disappearing. The boss is dead. And our institutions are in crisis.

More and more of our laws are unenforceable. Practically everyone is a scofflaw. Laws people perceive as an enforced code of behavior are simply ignored.

"Children have outgrown their schools," says James Coleman. But that is merely a special case of a nearly universal phenomenon. We are, all of us, outgrowing all our institutions.

Eighty-five percent of our young people subscribe to the statement: "Whether I work for government or business, I would like a job where I am more or less my own boss." But our institutions were not built for people who want to boss themselves.

At the turn of the century, Frederick Winslow Taylor, the prophet of "scientific management" and the godfather of all the hated time-study men, believing that people liked to be used efficiently, reduced production line tasks to an absurd, deadening simplicity. But Taylor's premise is obsolete. People will not be used at all.

And that isn't all. The world has changed. And change has brought with it problems of an order that simply can't be solved by authoritarian methods.

Highly structured, authoritarian, bureaucratic organizations were able to function passably well in a simpler world. But they cannot keep up with change. They cannot digest diversity, and our society is becoming almost incomprehensively diverse.

Marshall McLuhan believes we are now living "200

years per annum." "When you are moving at that clip," he says, "there is no place to stand. No job or organization chart will contain you. No management can hold its own at electric speeds. It is like putting a Model T on a highway at 100 mph. It breaks down."

America is, at least apparently, becoming unmanageable.

# 4

# The New American Dilemma

We enacted all the supposed remedies for all the great domestic problems . . . and they haven't worked . . . Now it gets very hard to fight . . . *For God's sake, give me something to be enthusiastic about.*

—Joseph Alsop

The obsolescence of authority has created a new American dilemma of historic proportions. Because, while it is clear that authority doesn't work anymore, we also believe that the world won't work without it. The apparent alternative to authority is chaos. Authority seems to be indispensable and unworkable at the same time.

Charles Reich's best seller, *The Greening of America*, describes the emerging unmanageable personality with a compelling eloquence, and calls it Consciousness III. Toward the end of the book, Reich asks rhetorically if Consciousness III can "actually do the necessary work of the world?" Will Consciousness III collect the garbage and run the railroads? Reich seems to believe it will. But most of the rest of the world flatly believes it can't. Dr. Frank Knopfelmacher, of the University of Melbourne, expressed the doubts of millions when he wrote in the *Wall Street Journal*:

If the Reich ideology were to prevail . . . we might yet see the "greening" of America, since the grass might grow where the machines of civilization once stood. . . . And life would again become solitary, poor, nasty, brutish and short.

American intellectuals were outraged by Reich's book, not because they thought he was wrong, but because they sensed he was dead right, and that the consequences would be catastrophic. Insubordinate Reichian students were destroying the tranquillity of their classrooms. Imagine them running U.S. Steel.

When the McDonagh School in Maryland decided to relax its military rules to attract more students, disturbed parents predicted "chaos by Christmas."

Rednecks sometimes shoot people with long hair. They see them as symbols of the coming chaos.

We believe we can't live with authority and we can't live without it. The public dialogue has become ambivalent to the point of absurdity. Politics has become inherently contradictory. Liberal and conservative ideologies have become irrelevant and trivial. A nation of people once known for its dogged optimism is in despair. Quackery and dishonesty flourish. Honest people can choose only between apathy, resignation or blind revolt. The American dream has become a lost cause. Our bicentennial celebration could be a wake.

Conservative thought is stale and passive. Liberal thought is hyperactive and naïve. Conservatives are appealing to a faith in freedom we never had. Liberals are appealing to a faith in government action we have lost.

When Elliot Richardson renounced HEW as unmanageable, he didn't go home. He went to the Pentagon to "run" a bureaucracy ten times bigger. The situation is Dadaistic. Richardson, a methodical man, tells the press the Department of HEW doesn't work. He carefully packs his portfolio, and is driven across town in a Cadillac to "run" the Department of Defense. One can imagine Peter Sellers playing the part and whistling on the way.

Richardson's behavior was sane and insane at the same time. It is beyond rational analysis. It will not compute. Bureaucracy doesn't work, but we cannot leave the nation undefended. We face a choice we cannot make.

And this is a special case of an emerging universal. We must choose between two equally unacceptable alternatives: (1) we can let the country go to hell, or (2) we can continue to try to fix it with methods we all know will fail. So we have programs and Presidents no one wants.

Ralph Nader, everybody's favorite reformer, becomes an advocate of the very methods he discredits. He must abandon either his idealism or his common sense. So he becomes big government's most effective critic and principal promoter—simultaneously. He stays sane, we must assume, by keeping one eye or the other tightly closed.*

Richard Nixon said, after the election: "It is time to get big government off your back and out of your pocket." A few weeks later he proposed the largest federal budget in the nation's history.

Politicians scarcely pretend to have solutions anymore.

* Nader, it must be said, is changing. After this was written, he told the Consumer Federation of America to "redirect their efforts away from legislation and strive instead for changes that would allow consumers to protect themselves without depending on government bureaucracies."

As national chairman of the McGovern–Shriver campaign, Lawrence O'Brien wrote an article in the *Wall Street Journal* a few days before the presidential election. Here is his diagnosis:

. . . . we have created a situation in which tens of millions of Americans—young, old, black, white, poor and rich—feel a deep discontent with the basic pattern of their lives. They feel that their inherent dignity as human beings is being squeezed in a tightening ring of big institutions—big schools, big business, big unions, big cities, big government—over which they have no control. . . . [they feel] that somehow we have taken the wrong path.

His prescription for change was less precise. We must, he said, "move ahead vigorously to do the things that must be done." He didn't say what things because he didn't know. O'Brien is a decent man, but he sounds like a snake-oil salesman.

When I first read this piece of O'Brien's, I was sitting in a doctor's office waiting for him to look at a rash on my shins. I could imagine the doctor saying, "You have somehow taken the wrong path, and now you must move ahead vigorously and do the things that must be done."

Professor John Kenneth Galbraith writes, "It would be foolish to suggest that government . . . is a good custodian of aesthetic goals." But, he concludes, "there is no alternative to the state."

One way to deal with the unconscionable is to laugh it off. A literature of light-hearted resignation has become popular. *Parkinson's Law* and *The Peter Principle* were best sellers.

*Washington Post* columnist David Broder writes that we are "confused about what we want from government, and so we contrive to give our public servants such conflicting signals that they can do anything they please—or nothing at all."

In January 1973 a Gallup poll showed that 54 percent of the public favored holding down spending for social programs. The next day a Harris poll showed clear majorities favoring more federal spending for pollution control and education, and to help the poor.

The press chose to call Nixon's victory in 1972 a landslide. But in spite of the most vigorous effort in history to get people to the polls dead or alive, and on a clear day from coast to coast, nearly half the nation stayed home. It was, if anything, a landslide for apathy, a historic victory for political indifference. It was as if we had listlessly elected a caretaker until our complaints could be more precisely diagnosed.

Theodore White keeps reporting how our Presidents are made. But even he now doubts the relevance of the process he has watched carefully for a lifetime: "This country has lost confidence in itself and in its destiny. . . . We've run out of ideas. . . . The governing ideas of America no longer fit the reality of American life."

Eight "experts" on public opinion including George Gallup and Daniel Yankelovich met in New Jersey. They described the nation's mood with words like "impotence," "lethargy," "resignation," "frustration," "disillusionment" and "chaos."

In Hartford, Connecticut, Tom Parrish, a Black service-station operator, says, "The Black man has given up on the system. He hates it. Now he's doing for himself and to hell with the system."

In Lorain, Ohio, Larry McGough, a thirty-year-old auto worker says: "There's no way to move, and there's no way to change it. You're just locked in until the day you die. . . ."

Delbert S. Elliott, a professor of sociology at the University of Colorado, sums it up: "People are frustrated with institutions from the top of the federal government on down . . . They've come to understand that the institutions are running things, and that they're beyond the control of individuals. So people are just giving up."

Our young people have given up the passion for reform that moved them in the sixties. "I tried for two years," says one, "and saw it was impossible to change things."

Even the Revolution has lost its appeal. "What for?" asks a teenage girl in New Jersey. "Who wants a messy revolution that just sets up another government that's self-serving to those who brought it about?"

A Japanese intellectual, Jonosuki Nagai, tells his people that to imitate America is to imitate disaster. "The United States is becoming a . . . nation without a unified general will . . . American institutions have lost their ability to restore themselves . . . America . . . has fallen into a vicious circle of frustration and distrust."

Opinion researcher Jay Schmiedeskamp says, "In our consumer confidence surveys, we ask people whether they think government economic policy is good, fair, or poor. Increasingly, the answer we get is just plain laughter."

A third of our college students say they would rather live somewhere else.

Where were the activist liberals when their country was in a final crisis? They were protesting the plight of people who pick lettuce. And the conservative activists? They were, when I could find them at all, trying to get liberalized abortion laws repealed.

The situation is dangerous. B. F. Skinner's book, chillingly titled *Beyond Freedom and Dignity*, was a best seller. Maybe, says Skinner, we can make men manageable again, using techniques he developed teaching pigeons to play ping-pong. And the idea suddenly appeals to a freedom-loving people.

But, happily, the coin has another, brighter side.

# Part II
# The Discovery of Another America

# 5

# America as Oz

It was the best of times; it was the worst of times.
—Charles Dickens

While America's institutions seemed to be failing, the people of America did not, strangely, perceive themselves as failing.

Many were living longer, happier, deeper, richer, healthier lives. They were learning more about themselves and their world. They were overcoming prejudices about each other. They were searching for and finding new levels of intimacy with each other. They had higher expectations for themselves than ever before, but, even so, perceived themselves as making solid progress.

Reporters who worked conventionally from vantage points in New York or Washington had nearly all joined the chorus of despair. But reporters who journeyed through America came back with another story altogether. Charles Kuralt, a TV broadcaster who traveled all over America to film his *On the Road* features, wrote in shocked recognition of that experience:

To read the papers and to listen to the news. . . . one would think the country is in terrible trouble. You do not get that impression when you travel the back roads and the small towns. . . . You find people who are courteous and neighborly and who really do care about their country and wish it well. . . . You do not get the feeling of a country on the brink of revolution or torn apart by hatred—the kind of impression you might get if you only read the page-one stories.

In 1971 Potomac Associates, working with the Gallup Organization, produced a pioneering study called *The Hopes and Fears of the American People*. It confirmed Kuralt's casual observation in a more systematic way. In their *personal* lives, Americans were, on the whole, contented. They told the pollsters that their lives were pretty good, rather better than they had been five years before. And they confidently expected their lives to become even more satisfying in the next five years. But a near majority of the same people thought the country was going to the dogs. "Almost one in every two Americans," the study's authors summarized, "sees tensions serious enough to lead to a real breakdown in this country."

The study was repeated in 1972 and 1974 with about the same result, revealing what the authors called "a bifurcated mood of personal progress but national doubt." And by 1975 a fear of economic collapse was becoming epidemic.

How can this be? How can we be failing and succeeding at the same time? How can we be succeeding individually and failing collectively? Clearly, if we are to make sense of the American experience, we need to find a new way of looking at it.

Professor Galbraith took a step in this direction in *The Affluent Society*. His thesis—that there was a perverse tendency for us to spend too much money on personal indulgences, such as cold cream, and too little on public necessities, such as research grants for college professors— was unconvincing. But the more basic idea—that there are really two Americas, that there are two conflicting dimensions to the American experience—is fundamental. America has to be looked at through bifocals to be understood.

Michael Harrington, a few years later, in *The Other America*, took another cut at it, and described a forgotten America under the elevated tracks which no one had seen very clearly before. And this idea, that there are invisible foreign lands inside our borders, is elemental.

But how are we to make the separation? What part of America is working and what part failing?

Years ago I worked for a while in a rusty little makeshift oil refinery in east Los Angeles. Most of us who worked there were leftovers from the war, disabled because of some deviance. We were crippled or female or too young or too old. There was Buck, the doleful alcoholic foreman who had concealed his addiction from the bosses for twelve troubled years. There was a quiet man we called simply "Pipe-fitter" who spoke only when something was on fire. There was young Howie who stole more oil than he canned. There was a kindly Mexican sweeper, whose brains had been scrambled forever when a drum hoist crashed on his head and who cried for days when Howie went to war.

There was an aging homosexual still-man who would stamp his foot when the steam pressure failed and spoiled his "batch"—as if his soufflé had fallen. There was gorgeous Loree, who laughed while she drove the rest of us crazy in skintight Levis.

But together we somehow made the plant work.

Every once in a while a nervous little man from the front office—with rimless glasses and a white shirt and a clipboard—would tiptoe through the pools of oil in the yard with some insane suggestion about how we could can oil faster. And Buck would bellow and chase him back where he belonged with a pipe wrench. This manager was probably a nice, earnest and conscientious man. He knew how to write reports and balance the books and make sales projections. But he didn't know anything about the delicate human harmony we had worked out together in the back. He didn't know that Buck had to be left all alone sometimes. He didn't know that only nonverbal communication worked with Pipe-fitter. He didn't know that if you spoke too sharply to the still-man, he would pout on his catwalk for a week and blend no oil. He didn't know that if you pestered Loree when she was menstruating she might break the Bowser (a device that dispenses measured amounts of fluid into containers) and that it would take Buck one shift to sober up so his hands wouldn't shake and two more to fix it again.

A lot of confusion is cleared if we look separately at "front-office America," "official America"—all the entities that in one way or another presume to manage or "run" the country or its institutions—and at the real experiential, unmanaged daily life of the people.

This is not to say that front-office America has no effect on unmanaged America. The two worlds are so hopelessly scrambled together that they can only be separated in the imagination.

Nevertheless, unmanaged America is a powerful reality, with its own mysterious metabolism. And once in a while we can see it working.

If you live in New York City and spend any time thinking about it, you find yourself wondering sometimes how the city works at all. But sometimes you feel a surging sense of awe that it works as well as it does.

Several years ago Michael Quill, head of the Transport Workers Union, having at last gathered all the transport workers into one invincible coalition, struck New York. All the public transport except one little bus line in Queens stopped running. But practically all of us got to work, some on bicycles, some roller-skating down the middle of Fifth Avenue, some crowding cheerfully into the few cabs that were operating, and many in more mysterious ways. But after the first day, almost no one missed work.

A couple of years later all New York's policemen quit working. New York was left officially unguarded. Sociologists have been puzzling ever since over the fact that there was no perceptible increase in crime during that uneasy period.

When George Romney was Secretary of the Department of Housing and Urban Development, he spent millions on a program he called Operation Breakthrough, a search for ways to build houses cheaply in factories—the way cars are built. Long before Operation Breakthrough was conceived, hundreds of thousands of houses were being built in factories. They had to be called "mobile homes," and ceremonial wheels were attached to them, to evade prehistoric zoning and building-code restrictions. But they were houses. They were built in factories. They were a lot cheaper than handmade houses. And millions of Americans were living in them happily while Romney was talking breathlessly to the press about Operation Breakthrough.

Everyone in Oz knew that Oz was run by a wonderful all-powerful wizard. When Dorothy and her friends finally found their way into the wizard's inner sanctum, something went wrong, and the screen fell down. The wizard, it turned out, was just a funny frightened old man from Kansas with a roomful of noisemakers and smoke machines. He had no real power at all. He didn't run Oz. He only seemed to. And suddenly the inhabitants realized that all the wizard's magical accomplishments were their own doing.

Right after World War II, I worked for a couple of months on a crew building tacky tract houses in the San Fernando Valley. The management gave us an absurdly detailed set of plans and instructions about how each house was to be built. We called it the "funny paper" and sometimes, if we could find it, we read it for laughs at lunch. We built the houses and drew our pay. I suppose our supervisor thought there was some causal connection between what we did and the instructions he gave us. But it was largely an illusion. His supervision was, on the whole, gratuitous and perfunctory.

Bennett Kremen writes in *The New York Times* about "doubling up," an illicit, worker-devised practice at Chevrolet's Vega assembly plant in Lordstown, Ohio. It is simple. Lordstown assemblers have found they can do better work if they work twice as fast half of the time and rest the other half. So they form themselves into teams of two. One member works furiously for half an hour while the other rests. Then they switch. They "double up." But doubling up is against the rules. It isn't the way the front office has decided the work is supposed to be done. So workers have to double up on the sly. "If someone comes around," says Dave McGarvey, "we just put our hand on the car. We just play the game with him." The foremen are torn. They are paid to see that assemblers go by the book. But they also want to keep production and quality up. So "quite a few" foremen simply disappear. They "go over to the other line for a Coca-Cola." Replacement operator Joe Alfona adds, "The guys know what they mean. They'll do a good job for that foreman."

The unmanaged assembly line works better. Smart foremen get results by refusing to interfere.

We live with the illusion that America is run by its front offices. The president, we say, runs the country. Abe Beame runs New York. Henry Ford runs the Ford Motor Company. The reality is that these elaborate structures do not run the country. They only seem to. We believe in a myth, that America works because it is managed. The opposite is much closer to the truth. What works in America works in spite of the expensive, elaborate and increasingly destructive efforts to manage it.

Right now there are more managers than producers in America. In 1950, according to Karl Hess, fourteen million people in America were working in the front office as clerks, managers, officials or proprietors, and twenty-two million were doing real work. By 1970 the front-office establishment had swollen to twenty-one million and the number of producers had dwindled to eighteen million. In other words, the managers now outnumber the managed.

The number of people who escape management by working on their own has declined drastically. Twenty years ago there were five million self-employed people in America. Today there are only a million. Signs of stagnation and atrophy are everywhere. Capital for financing new enterprises has shrunk in a similar way.

America, viewed in terms of the intentions and activities of the front office, is a failure. But unofficial America, underground America, unmanaged America, to the decreasing degree it can escape the control of the front office, still shows unmistakable signs of vitality.

The two Americas are strangely separate worlds. In 1973 John De Lorean suddenly quit his $550,000-a-year job with General Motors. "GM," he said, "has gotten to be a total insulation from the realities of the world."

Front-office America sees unmanaged America as a stubborn, shapeless, unruly mass that must be endlessly molded and motivated—managed. Unmanaged America calls front-office America "the establishment" and hates it for its dishonesty and arrogance and presumption.

A white Southern workingman told Robert Coles: "I don't believe ninety percent of what they say. I guess they look down on the ordinary workingman. I guess they don't trust us. I guess they figure they can con us, all the time con us."

So it is no wonder we are confused.

We probably know too much about front-office America, but we know hardly anything about unmanaged America. Its activities are largely unknown and unreported.

# 6

# Our One-
# Eyed Press

Enter a priest disguised as a priest.
—A stage instruction in an Elizabethan play

The superstition that America works because the front office manages it is reinforced every day by what we read in the papers.

The American press is a front-office press. It reports America as if it were Oz, as if what is remarkable about society are the efforts to manage it. The more remote and authoritarian an institution, the more likely the press is to report its activities exhaustively. As a result, we are strangers to our own society.

The press gives more space to the intentions of authority than to the accomplishments of unofficial America. It outrageously overreports politics and thus perpetuates the illusion that political action is our principal engine of change and reform.

One would think, reading the papers and news magazines, that front offices run the country. For example, the activities of the New York police department are reported extensively in the New York papers. The assumption is, of course, that what the police do is the principal cause of increases or decreases in crime rates.

When someone pointed out that there was no perceptible increase in crime during New York's famous police strike, the *Times* carried a bewildered little article noting the fact—but that was the end of it. Researchers have experimentally quadrupled the number of patrolmen in certain precincts while eliminating patrols entirely in others. It makes no difference. This means, of course, that something else is at work—that some unknown force or process has more effect on crime than do the activities of the police. But the press does not pursue the matter. It continues to report dutifully the changes in the politics and practices of the police department, as if they were of some special importance. There are now, for example, more privately paid than publicly paid policemen in America. But the activities of the private police are hardly ever mentioned in the papers.

A couple of years ago Congress established a Commission on Product Safety and appointed a commissioner. Suddenly, product safety was news. The new commissioner got luxurious coverage when he announced simply that he was going to seek news coverage.

For nearly a hundred years, thousands of people, working through a couple of dozen independent organizations—Underwriters Laboratories, the American Fire Protection Association, the American National Standards Institute—have been dealing with product safety with a rare persistence and imagination. Thousands of standards have been developed, millions of tests conducted. This less official activity was hardly ever reported. The press discovered product safety only when the federal government decided to manage it.

When President Kennedy announced that he was going to form a Peace Corps and send a few hundred young people overseas, the event and the subsequent activities of the Peace Corps were reported exhaustively. At the time Kennedy made the announcement, at least thirty-three thousand Americans were working abroad as volunteers doing the same things in the same countries that the Peace Corpsmen were then only talking about. I never saw a word in the daily press about this unofficial effort. Overseas volunteering did not become real to the working press until it became official.

The last time I checked, VISTA, the domestic Peace Corps, was supporting about six thousand young people in American communities. The total number of Americans who work as volunteers through less official agencies may exceed seventy million. But while VISTA's activities are reported systematically, the activities of the others are rarely mentioned.

What is happening in the hearts of millions of women is probably the most permanent and far-reaching change in American society in this generation. It has solved the population "problem." As soon as sensible birth control devices became widely available, women, having already discovered in themselves capacities beyond childbearing, began to use the new methods—when the front office allowed them to. In about a decade, women had themselves reduced the population growth rate to zero—the only serious, measurable social accomplishment of the period.

But that was the least of it. Women's fuller sense of what and who they are is altering the daily lives of all of us. It is leading men and women to open their hearts to each other in ways they have rarely done before. It has changed the atmosphere in practically every work place in America. It is revolutionizing family life. But not much of this is reportable by customary methods, and is thus largely ignored.

The press is a kind of collective house organ for the front office. It is in no way an accurate mirror of America. It reports as real one half-mythical aspect of the American experience, and hints sometimes at the existence of another, unknown, unmanaged America.

The *Wall Street Journal* and its weekend cousin, the *National Observer,* do, for some reason, give us glimpses of unmanaged America better than most. Here you can read about the people of America, sense the seething infinite diversity—clowns and barbed-wire collectors, and steeple-jacks and silversmiths. But even then, unmanaged America is presented as something alien and unfamiliar, as one might report Bantu tribal rites.

It is a common complaint that the press is biased. Conservatives say the press has a liberal bias—and are forever starting little papers and magazines to set the record straight. Liberals say the press has a conservative bias and have their own little magazines to report the truth.

But the most serious problem is not so much bias as defective, selective vision, and an obsession with authority. The problem is largely inherent: gathering news from movie stars and people in power is a comparatively effortless business. Authority performs for the press. The front office is desperately—sometimes exclusively—concerned with appearances, and with the perpetuation of the management illusion.

The first question in the halls of authority is "How will it look?"—by which is meant "What will the reporters say about it?" Then the press dutifully reports as news what the front office has already decided would be news. It isn't a conspiracy, exactly, but it works like one.

When I was at NAM, everything we did, we did for the press. NAM existed exclusively for the press and was, in turn, a product of the press. NAM, a result of front-office mythology if there ever was one, was, in a sense, an illusion. It had no reality beyond the artificial news it created.

The press reports what is most readily reportable—beauty contests and prizefights and elections and other similar barbarities. Thus it has made the synthetic seem authentic and left the authentic unreported.

You can put it down as a kind of law that the most important happenings have no spokesmen, no office of public relations, and hence no voice that is intelligible to the working press.

It is no wonder Americans are puzzled. The press can only report what is visible and vocal. The only part of America it knows how to report is failing. The part that is succeeding is unreported.

# 7

# The Price
# of Management

The growth of affluence, the growth of education, has led to
a shortage of morons.
                                    —Leonard Neal
                                    British industrial relations expert

I had a professor in college who told me incessantly that we
had in our wisdom created a society that was greater than
the sum of its parts—that the efforts of the members of
society are somehow magically enhanced and magnified by
the institutions they work through. I had trouble getting my
mind around this idea, and I still do.

A society should be at least as good as the sum of the
potential of its parts, but our society is not. Our reliance on
management has produced a society that is less than it could
be. We are collectively much less than we are individually.
Management suppresses and limits, diminishes the quality
and quantity of our human responses.

A good society is one that not only permits but
welcomes the full expression of all the human qualities of
the people who are part of it—one in which all the willing

energy of all its members can be fully involved. A society that uses people partly or perversely is underproductive. A society that finds ways to involve everybody fully becomes superproductive.

Inventions which engage masses of people in any productive process have extraordinary results. Small contrivances can have huge consequences. We tremble when we hear about inventions that displace people. But the crucial inventions are of an opposite order, those that *involve* more people more fully in the world's work.

The use of carts on wheels in grocery stores revolutionized retailing by deprofessionalizing the process—democratizing it—and involving millions of shoppers in selecting and fetching merchandise.° There are many such inventions: sewing machines, fire extinguishers, watches, dial telephones, vending machines, typewriters, hand cameras, home freezers and a hundred more. They break down some prior technical aristocracy, and let everybody into the act.

I once bought what had been a "slave" clock. It was wired into a "master" clock and simply relayed the time. The slave clock was useless by itself—wholly dependent. But a Bleecker Street clocksmith fitted it with works of its own, and now it is independent—it works by itself.

Movable type was an emancipating, democratizing invention. In time it brought papers and books into everyone's hands and undermined the tyranny of the intellectual elite. The invention of the stock corporation meant that the nickels and dimes of masses of people could be invested in businesses, and the productiveness of enterprise was greatly multiplied.

° Grocers often exploit this involvement, cynically arranging their merchandise so that it is much easier to waste money than to save it.

The sheer power of masses of people is awesome. We tend to think of our society as being much more top-heavy than it really is because the antics of the rich and famous are so generously reported. We forget that the really formidable productive power is in the accumulated energy of large numbers of people.

I have sometimes tried to imagine what the practice of medicine would be like without the thermometer. It is a simple inexpensive device that involves millions of people in diagnosing sickness.

Inventions are only one vivid way in which participation can be extended. The practice of medicine is being revolutionized not so much by supersophisticated devices for superspecialists, but by people's widening interest in and capacity for self-care. Women, particularly, are learning how their bodies work and are treating themselves, thus becoming free of the clumsy tyranny of the gynecologists. People are learning law and representing themselves in simple legal matters—uncontested divorces, uncomplicated real estate transactions and the like.

The most difficult educational task of all is teaching our infant children to speak our impossible language. It isn't accomplished by a handful of technicians, but almost unconsciously by millions of fond, involved parents.

But the numbers of people involved in the world's work represent only one raw dimension. More important is the quality of their involvement. And authority is the enemy of such involvement.

A couple of years ago I spent a day in a plastic-molding plant on the outskirts of Chicago. It was in a huge old brick building, one of those decaying structures you see from the elevated highways and wonder what goes on inside.

I first spent some time in the front office, looking at the books and at samples of the extraordinary variety of plastic forms people produced there—bobbins and frames for glasses, intricate miniature insulators, huge housings for computer tapes and hundreds more.

After a while, I got a badge and permission to wander through the plant. In time, in a forgotten corner, I encountered a young woman solemnly attending a giant plastic-molding machine. Every few seconds, the machine would clank and spit out a plastic form that looked like a cover for a large cake plate. The young woman would take the part, spin it skillfully around in her gloved hand, and then add it to an enormous pile that surrounded and nearly engulfed her.

She turned off her machine and we talked. She told me matter-of-factly that her job was really very simple. She was to take each new molding off the machine and to look at it carefully. If she saw no flaw, she was to pack it in a cardboard carton. If she saw any imperfection—a bubble or a crack or a bulge—the molding was to be tossed in a rubbish bin. She was puzzled only because the rubbish bin the management had supplied was so small and had overflowed so long ago. The machine had not produced a passable cake plate for ever so long. But she was comfortably and confidently doing exactly what she had been told to do.

A child would know that the machine was broken. But the young woman had been subhumanly programmed and was confidently—almost stubbornly—playing out the animal role some impatient production engineer had assigned to her. I could imagine her shutting down the machine when the whistle blew, gossiping with her friends at lunch, and then returning to produce a few hundred more useless objects before suppertime.

Such insanities are commonplace in a managed society, and the cost is enormous. This case was special only because the result was palpable, visible as a mountain of useless plastic moldings.

Having talked with this young woman, I would guess that something less than one percent of her human capacities was engaged by her assignment—and that, perversely. But in every managed institution in America, millions of carefully programmed people are wasting themselves and their time in aimless and perverse activities.

In 1967, about a year after I joined NAM, I attended a conference on women at Notre Dame. It was the first time I had been around emancipated women in any numbers. I was then dimly aware of a women's liberation movement, but I must have thought it contended simply that men should help with the housework. But as I listened I began to see the issue much more clearly. In those three days I came to realize that I was a classic male chauvinist by training and temperament, and that because of this, my life and the lives of the women in it had been much less satisfying than they might have been. I did not feel guilty—only deprived and sad. The "roles" to which an insane, authoritarian convention had assigned women were severely limiting, and women had been misshapen by them.

But men were crippled too—only in a different way. I had never seen so clearly before what awful human damage can be done by institutions that are unsuitable to the human beings who have to live in them. In any human relationship where power is present, someone is dominant and someone is subordinate. The subordinate party tends to be diminished, the dominant party corrupted, and both are made less human.

It dawned on me at South Bend that there was a striking parallel between the status of women and the status of practically all of us. Almost everyone has been diminished by some authoritarian superstition.

Such superstitions are commonplace in our society:

*Women* are empty-headed, hysterical and unreliable. They make sense only in combination with an authoritarian male. Their place is in the home. They are malcontents and complain incessantly.

*Schoolchildren* are lazy and mischievous and resist learning ferociously. They must be compelled to go to school, watched vigilantly and forced to learn by stern negative incentives.

*Adolescents* are irresponsible, unfit for serious responsibility. They must be watched carefully and locked into their rooms at night. They are prone to debauchery. They are sex-crazed and self-destructive. They must be deprived of stimulants, depressants, firearms and pictures of naked people.

*Employees* are lazy, dishonest and rebellious. They would rather not work at all and work best when they are terror-stricken. They have no imagination. They must be carefully instructed how to perform the simplest task.

*People in general* are larcenous, insensitive to the needs of others, hopelessly narcissistic. They are given to reckless driving, indecent exposure and defacing public monuments. They are stupid except when they vote.

*Businessmen* are greedy, crooked, base and unscrupulous. Their natural inclinations are to produce shabby or poisonous merchandise and overcharge for it. They must be watched vigilantly or they will kill half the population and bankrupt the rest.

*Consumers* are ignorant and gullible. They cannot tell a rotten apple from a good one. They believe everything they hear, and give particular weight to what they hear on television. Their most urgent appetites are for the things that are least good for them. Left to themselves, they would squander their wages on cotton candy, costume jewelry, dirty movies and fortune tellers.

And thus we have developed in families and factories, schools and offices, practices designed to correct these hypothetical failings but which in fact produce and perpetuate them.

Our institutions make us less than we could be. So there are enormous backlogs of vitality, caring, ingenuity and humanity which cannot be expressed through our present social machinery. That is the price we pay for allowing society to be managed.

And management works only to the degree that people can be persuaded or conditioned to accept these definitions of themselves.

The Army is the most extreme example of methodical dehumanization. Signs of individuality are painstakingly erased. Men are put in uniform so they will seem the same. They are taught to act mechanically, like the interchangeable parts of a bicycle. The perfect soldier is a robot. With a few, the dehumanization process works almost completely. Sensing this, we are inclined to forgive soldiers who murder women and children.

The Army works. It works with an awful inefficiency, but it works. Because it utilizes only the animal capacities of its participants, an extraordinary support apparatus is necessary to compensate for the assumed absence of human qualities. There are between five or six staff bureaucrats to care for, feed, direct and discipline each soldier in the field. Moving an Army around the world is like moving a huge menagerie of helpless, dangerous animals.

All managed institutions are more or less like the Army. Their essential error is that they adapt the plausible principles of engineering to human enterprises, by defining roles or tasks for people or institutions which are based on false or incomplete notions or prejudices of what they could be or do. But engineering deals with inert, largely predictable, tractable, manageable material. Management deals with people. And there is an elemental difference between a person and a bar of iron which management must ignore in order to "work."

Industry "structures" its jobs so they can be performed by people who can't think. "The difficulty," writes management consultant David Sirota, "is that normal human beings are usually hired to fill these jobs."

Philosophically we believe that each person is absolutely unique, irreplaceable. But in our managed institutions we try to treat people as interchangeable, and complain when they don't act that way.

The way we teach students, for example, is logical, if teaching is viewed as an engineering problem. Our methods make sense when they are applied to adding information to the memory of a computer. We translate the message into a form we know the computer can comprehend, transmit it by a method we know will alter the computer's memory, and then test, by asking the computer questions, to be sure the transmission was truly recorded. This is how we teach children and it doesn't work. Only a fraction of the child's human capacity is involved in the process.

And so, to some degree—as wives, or students, or children, or employees or subjects of government—we are diminished. We have all been housebroken, or trained or oriented to act out rigid, constricting roles. We do it because we believe society will come apart if we don't. We are corrupted by compliance. We believe that an unmanaged man is a menace.

American society is being disfigured by its institutions. Authority forces human material into unnatural shapes. Authority produces abundantly what presumably it exists to prevent—the maldistribution of responsibility. Misplaced responsibility drives out the competent. A person trapped by a limiting myth cannot readily go beyond it.

At NAM I once spent weeks working out a way to rearrange our offices so the space would be used somewhat sensibly. As things stood, the executives' offices occupied the whole outer perimeter of the building, and the remaining space was largely wasted.

But the plan I worked out was never considered, and I innocently pestered my fellow managers to act on it or at least discuss it. Finally, an older hand carefully closed the door to my office and explained to me furtively that my floor plan had a disabling flaw. "The women," he whispered, "have windows."

"Jobs are just not big enough for people," says Norma Watson, a writer and editor. "A monkey could do what I do," says Sharon Atkins, a receptionist with a college degree in English literature. "You're nothing but a machine," says Phil Stallings who makes 12,288 welds a day at a Chicago auto plant. An adman talks about his fellow admen: "They're talking about little bears running around a cereal box and arguing which way the bears should go. It's a silly thing for adults to be doing." *

Common sense tells us that some people are dangerous and need restraint. But that simple necessity does not mean that we all need to be told when we can go to the bathroom.

Perhaps half our social energy goes into vain and misguided efforts to manage the other half, creating a vast front-office establishment that is becoming daily more politicized and corrupt.

Authority cannot be fair. It produces the hustler, the image-maker, the bullshit artist. Ours is an age when the appearance of results is better than solid accomplishments. It is the age of "creative bookkeeping." It is the age of getting ahead in business without really doing anything.

It is an age of too many unenforceable regulations and too much energy spent in search of ways to evade them. Honorable men taught fair play on the playing fields of Exeter boast in their clubs about patently immoral stock deals—if they are legal.

It's a society with too many taxes, and too much energy spent in figuring out ways to avoid them.

The distribution of work has been politicized. Men are paid for idleness while their willing Black brothers wait in the street.

Education has become piously corrupt.

* These quotations are all taken from *Working*, Studs Terkel's magnificent collection of edited interviews with working people.

A nation of warm and friendly people are showing increasing hostility to each other.

Grown women are called girls and type in cubbyholes.

It's a world where only 10 percent of the violent crimes are solved and, hence, where those punished seem more guilty of bad luck than iniquity. Even so, prisoners are surprisingly content with their sentences. They are worried about gratuitous brutalities to which they were not sentenced and the awful, mysterious inequity of the parole process.

Manipulative management is producing a society that is sluggish, that provides real satisfaction in work only to a tiny minority who are somehow exempt from management. Manipulation produces tensions of two sorts: the discomfort that comes when people feel forced every day to be less than they could be; and the frustration we feel when we see the growing gap between what we could achieve collectively and what we do achieve.

**8**

# The Maldistribution of Public Responsibility

Whatever can go wrong will go wrong.

—Murphy

An organization works badly if it is managed by manipulation because it under-uses and misuses people. In the same way, a nation works badly if it is governed manipulatively because it under-uses or misuses its institutions.

We are getting deeply disappointing results in dealing with the public business, not so much because we don't know how to fill potholes or deliver mail or collect garbage, but because the process by which we assign responsibility for these jobs is perverse. The most a society can ask of itself is that responsibility flows to whatever organization is best able to take it. But this is not true in America.

Millions of indescribably diverse entities make up the American polity. There are, first of all, more than two hundred million people of all shapes and colors and ages and sizes. They are all different. These people have arranged themselves into a staggering diversity of ever-changing groups: families, block associations, giant international companies, governments, secret societies, research teams, car pools, crap games.

There are five thousand newsletters in America and at least one newsletter of newsletters. The dictionary of occupational titles weighs ten pounds. It lists, among thousands of other occupations, "ecdysiasts"—striptease dancers. There are several hundred barbed wire collectors and they have an association. There is a foundation devoted to developing a system of notation for the dance. There are at least a thousand clown clubs. There are a hundred thousand dwarfs in America and they have an association, the Little People of America, Inc. There are soapbox derbies and hunt clubs and county fairs. There are wild horse roundups and flower shows. There is an American Association for the Study of Headache. The man who just left my study is a political scientist. His father was a concert bandmaster. His uncle was a riverboat gambler. There are something like five million business enterprises, ranging from bootblacks and pushcart peddlers to giant multinational companies. There is a man in Florida who makes a living making microscope guides out of the webs of black-widow spiders. There are manufacturers of sealing wax and supersonic airplanes and tote boards and dental floss and hairpieces and space capsules.

The way the front office distributes responsibility among these myriad groups is perverse.

In the same way that an authoritarian office manager assigns roles to the people who work for him based on strange superstitions about their abilities, our legislatures confer responsibilities on institutions on the basis of prejudices that increasingly have no relation to reality.

For example, Congress has decreed that the U.S. Postal Service shall deliver all first-class letters. It is a crime for anyone else to do it. Now, it is doubtful whether a government agency will ever be very good at delivering mail. Wherever competition is legal, commercial organizations do a better job more cheaply. There are, of course, a lot of important things commercial organizations do not do very well, but, predictably, they are comparatively skillful at delivering letters and parcels. United Parcel Service has already won more than half the parcel business away from the Postal Service. UPS is cheaper. It picks up parcels, delivers them faster and in better shape. The Postal Service damage rate is five times that of UPS. "While we were reading regulation books and discouraging business," says Assistant Postmaster General Edgar S. Brower, "they were accommodating customers."

Partly by decree and partly by custom, schools have the overwhelming share of responsibility for teaching young people. This assignment is based on the nearly universal superstition that schools are effective at teaching. But there is mounting evidence that schooling—which, according to Ivan Illich, was conceived by an alchemist—doesn't work, that children learn much more much faster from each other, or from their parents or in other, more mysterious ways, than they do in school and that schools may stifle more curiosity than they satisfy. Some of the most learned people I know never set foot in a school. Their parents defied the law and taught them at home.

In some states, corporations cannot legally run hospitals or nursing homes.

In California, according to law, the state cannot buy any service that can conceivably be supplied by a state agency. For the state to contract with, say, a private employment service to find jobs for unemployed people would require a constitutional amendment.

We cannot legally bury our dead. We must hire a business to do it.

Ivan Illich reminds us that "most curable sickness can now be treated by laymen." But it is a crime for laymen to treat each other. A seventeen-year-old girl who treated a hundred and thirty of her classmates for venereal disease was arrested and tried. The judge let her go on a technicality when experts found she got far better results than the U.S. Public Health Service.

Until most of the states passed corrective "good Samaritan" laws, the law actively discouraged citizens from helping accident victims on the roadside.

In every session of every legislative body in the land, lawmakers continue to heap responsibility on cities, counties, states and federal bureaus with nothing but hunch and prejudice to guide them. A generation of this impulsive effort has given most government bodies more responsibilities than they can count, much less exercise.

There is a stubborn, nearly universal hunch that tax-based social programs are the only ones that really work, that a federal response to a public problem is always and necessarily a stronger, more responsible one.

This social chauvinism tends to imprison nonfederal institutions in a limiting definition, in the same way that women, having been socially defined as subordinate, *became* what they were prejudicially defined to be. Nonfederal institutions—regardless of their real potential—have been socially defined as inferior, and have had trouble growing beyond that limiting definition.

For years we made it practically impossible for women

to go to law school and then smugly pointed out that women obviously had limited capacity for practicing law because there were so few women lawyers.

For years we have encouraged the federal government to tax away money that would otherwise have nourished nonfederal institutions and then smugly pointed out that nonfederal institutions obviously had a waning capacity for social responsibility because they were taking less and less of it.

The sexual chauvinist sees women as physically weak and emotionally unstable and thus unfit for serious work. The social chauvinist sees nonfederal institutions, lacking the federal government's supreme power to tax and command, as incapable of taking serious social responsibility. Government—big and bold and boastful, like a locker-room bully—seems capable of anything it puts its mind to.

Deeply embedded in the conventional wisdom are certain limiting superstitions about our institutions:

*Local governments* are comparatively stupid, myopic and corrupt. They will spend money with abandon on a new courthouse, but will not fill the potholes.

*Voluntary agencies*° are timid, weak and unreliable. They can be trusted only with simple, unimportant tasks like maintaining dog cemeteries. Large or complicated problems are beyond their capacities.

*Commercial organizations* are all right for making steel and mouthwash, but they have no capacity for work that requires any subtlety or humanity. They

---

° Our neglected network of five million noncommercial, nongovernmental organizations.

cannot teach or keep the peace. They can deliver milk, but not mail. They can run hotels, but not hospitals.

*Families* are stupid and insensitive. They can be trusted with thermometers and Band-Aids, but with nothing more sophisticated. Any very serious need is best provided by more reliable agencies outside.

*Individuals* are ignorant and suicidal. They will not come in out of the rain without professional counsel and motivation. They are stubbornly indifferent to the possibilities for self-improvement. They must be strapped into moving vehicles.

And, for generations, we have assigned social roles on the basis of these doubtful suppositions. Our institutions have been trapped in limiting definitions, just as surely as Black Pullman porters or "girls" in secretarial pools.

On the other hand, we often simply confer competence on people and institutions in the same prejudiced way.

Teachers, for instance, are credentialed. They are competent by declaration. In junior high school I had a "social studies" teacher. He had the credentials to teach. He explained at the beginning of the course with a rare and admirable candor that he had no interest in teaching. Because he had tenure, he explained, he could be fired only for moral delinquency, and he had outgrown that capacity. His name was Jason Baker Wirsig.

We spent two luxurious semesters with JB, with our feet up, smoking, gossiping and thumbing through magazines in a marvelously relaxed barbershop atmosphere. It did no harm, surely. But the point is that JB was a "teacher" by proclamation. His status had nothing to do with what he did or accomplished, only what his credentials specified he was capable of doing. An educational result was presumed, but none took place. We accepted JB as a happy windfall, and loved him dearly. And our records all showed that we had "taken" social studies for a year in the tenth grade and were, in our turn, forever presumed to know something about it.

Colleges are accredited—a kind of institutional credentialing. But again the meaning is presumptive, methodically insulated from the world of results. Credentialing committees count books in the library, measure square feet of space, appraise laboratory equipment, examine fringe benefits, and review the credentials of the faculty. If this physical and human equipment conforms to a standard, a school or college is accredited—ordained—and can in turn grant credentials to its graduates.

Now, it is perfectly obvious that no education need take place in these accredited institutions. Probably a student would learn more in an evening with Betty Friedan than in a full semester in one of these expensive cathedrals of higher learning. But that is irrelevant. These institutions have been defined as educational, and we accept their product, inferentially, as education.

Fifteen years or so ago, working for a foundation that once in a while made a sentimental grant for cancer research, I came to know of a doctor pursuing a grisly superstition in northern Michigan. His name was Carruthers. His office wall was crowded with his credentials, displayed in gilt frames, some of them in Latin. He treated advanced cancer patients by injecting them with a substance, which, when analyzed, proved to be almond extract. His colleagues, themselves locked into the credentialing system, made no move to contain his mayhem, but privately they considered the man dangerously insane and called him "Crazy Carruthers." His patients all died, and only Carruthers was surprised. But he had been pronounced a healer. He had papers to prove it. So his activities were presumed to have a healing effect. And when statisticians calculated the nation's healing resources, Crazy Carruthers was surely among them.

I read the other day that the doctors had taken some steps to discipline the alcoholics and lunatics in their ranks, but I could not help wondering at the mentality that could so long postpone so obvious a reform.

We license policemen, dogcatchers, nurses, doctors, electricians. Bureaucracies ordain a man a facilitator, and presume that he facilitates when he may very well obstruct.

To compound the error, our legislatures assign mechanical procedures to institutions, in the same wrong-headed way that an authoritarian manager assigns procedures to the people who work for him.

Congress passes endless "programs." There is a farm program, a foreign-aid program, a poverty program, a housing program and literally thousands more—Professor Alfred de Grazia counted more than seven thousand federal programs in 1971. These programs are always more or less intricate sets of procedures, based on some fashionable conjecture. The government employees do what the law says. But their activities are disconnected from any final reality. From time to time, government programs are evaluated, found ineffective, and the program is somehow modified—and more often than not, enlarged. Procedures are changed, but they are still procedures. It is like a blind man shagging stones at a crow. Success is largely accidental.

I stood stunned and bleeding for forty minutes on a New York street last spring, watching a hundred empty cabs go by that could have taken me to the hospital twelve blocks away. But the policeman who had taken charge of me insisted menacingly that we wait for an ambulance. I half overheard a whispered conversation with his senior partner. The "book" didn't clearly permit the use of a "private conveyance" in the circumstances. So that was that. An unprogrammed eight-year-old would have known that the humanly sensible thing to do was to hail a cab. But the book had transformed my cop into a robot. He could move only in certain predetermined ways. He had been dehumanized, his common sense unplugged by a book of rules—as effective as a lobotomy. Had I bled to death waiting for an ambulance, I'm sure he would have slept soundly, peacefully confident that he had done what he was supposed to do.

Ordained procedures are practically immortal. Early in World War II, when Germany was prepared to fight and England wasn't, the British Army hastened to collect anything that would shoot in order to defend the English coast until more modern weapons could be built. They found a number of old cannons of a certain World War I type and prepared to put them back into service. As they reviewed the manual for firing the weapon, they were puzzled. At one point, the firing procedure was suspended for several seconds while two members of the gun crew left their places, walked a few paces aside and stood at attention. Then the firing drill continued. The maneuver seemed aimless to the reviewing officers but they were loath to eliminate it, thinking, I suppose, that it had some important invisible purpose. So they disturbed the retirement of an old gunner, brought him to the testing ground, and put the gun crew through the drill. "What are they doing?" they asked, as the action stopped and the two crewmen drew aside and snapped to attention. "It's very simple," the old man replied, "they're holding the horses."

In one of his budget messages, President Nixon proposed to abolish the federal Board of Tea Experts, which meets once a year to taste tea. I watched the issue carefully. I knew of only two peacetime federal programs that had been abandoned: stabling stallions for breeding cavalry horses and distilling rum in the Virgin Islands. Now it seemed there might be a third. But a few weeks later, the government retreated. The tea tasters were reappointed and the appropriation continued.

So millions of numbered bureaucrats sit in assigned places to perform assigned tasks. Everything they do is plausible at the level of conjecture. They work hard and by the book.

Our social problems seethe and fester while millions of these nice people are doing exactly what they are told to do, and wondering at night why everyone is so hostile to bureaucracy. Our wars against social pathologies are looking-glass wars. But the bureaucrat is innocent. He has been sent to hunt bears with a switch.

The error is elemental. Social management doesn't work.

The longer people stay in school the worse they write. Unschooled five-year-olds write with a marvelous directness and simplicity: "I got out of my bed and put on my socks." Most graduate dissertations are nearly incomprehensible.

There is, according to Gordon Tullock, an *inverse* correlation between the measurable output of a consulate and the number of "qualified" professionals assigned to it.

I can detect a tendency, when authority assigns social tasks, for responsibility to flow to the person or agency *least* likely to handle it competently. I am not altogether sure why this might be so, but I am tempted to follow the lead of Professors Parkinson and Peter and promulgate a law of my own: "Authority tends to assign jobs to those least able to do them."

Here are some frivolous examples. In many parts of the Catholic world, celibate priests have the major responsibility for dispensing birth control information. For a time during the Kennedy administration, Pierre Salinger was the nation's most visible promoter of physical fitness. During the Democratic Convention in 1968, Richard Daley was mainly responsible for dealing with the angry young people who came to Chicago.

But there are many more serious examples: People who run prisons are mainly responsible for teaching prisoners how to live in peace outside prisons. The federal government, which spends more money than it collects three years in four, is responsible for maintaining the integrity of our monetary system. The U.S. Employment Service, which pays people who are not working, has a large responsibility for helping people find work. The New York City government, surely America's sloppiest institution, is mainly responsible for keeping New York clean. Steve Savas, when he was first deputy city administrator, found it cost the city three times as much to collect a ton of garbage as it costs the private carters who collect garbage for a fee from the city's restaurants and hotels.

Americans now pay $1.15 of every $3.00 they earn to pay for the repetition of thousands of discredited procedures. The results are more than just irritating. They have led to a galloping disaffection with American society, the destruction of our cities, surging inflation, impending economic collapse, and, most of all, to a creeping sense of national impotence and despair.

But the cause is not very widely understood. So there is a preoccupation with two plausible remedies—one very old and one very new.

The first is to make government businesslike. Every decade or so, there is a major effort to reform the workings of government. In the recent past, there was a Hoover Commission, followed by another. Nixon, noting that Hoover was dead, asked Roy Ash, president of Litton Industries, to head what came to be known as the Ash Commission.

What we remember about these commissions is that they labored long and sensibly, that they produced elaborate recipes for reform, that the President and Congress acted favorably on their recommendations, and that the bureaucracies hastened to comply. What is forgotten is that six months later the results of these mighty and conscientious labors are imperceptible. Government does not cost less and work better. It costs more and works less well. Government is forever reorganizing itself, like a restless sleeper, thinking always that a new position will be more comfortable than the last. Efficiency commissions simply compound the initial transgression. There is no end to the aimless improvements that can be made to an appliance that is not plugged in.

More recently, another approach has come into fashion. It is proposed that we apply high technology to the problems of our streets and cities. The idea is captivating. If we put a man on the moon, we ask, why can't we make the streets safe at night?

But there is no real connection between the two enterprises. One is an engineering problem; the other is not. One might as well ask, "If we can build a light bulb that will burn forever, why can't we make life eternal?" The two ambitions are of a wholly different order.

But when the Apollo 15 astronauts came back, President Nixon told Congress, "Let us find the means to insure that . . . the remarkable technology that took these Americans to the moon can also be applied to reaching our goals here on earth." The bureaucrats began breathlessly to compile a list of possibilities: cable TV for remote medical diagnosis, enriched diet-improving soda pop, computerized traffic lights and the like.

We assume that what is wrong with our public services is our technique, which can be corrected like a ragged golf swing. But the problem is not to create new transcendent technologies but to discover why we are not using the humbler technologies we already know—or even why we use so rarely the most prosaic and useful technology of all, which is common sense. Otherwise we will simply add to the frustrating backlog of technique we fail to apply. Some doctors are saying, for example, that the space age machinery is interfering with sensible medical practice.

The basic problem is not a lack of know-how. We are trying to improve society by managing it—and our kind of management doesn't work.

# Part III
# Alternatives to Authority

# 9

# Our Backward Social Sciences

I think the greatest curse of American society has been the idea of an easy millennialism—that some new drug, or the next election or the latest in social engineering will solve everything.

—Robert Penn Warren

The assumption that people and institutions can be methodically arranged and activated—managed—is subliminal to most social thought.

Social scientists tend to be meddlesome, mechanistic and authoritarian. Thus the social science textbooks our children bring home from school describe a mythical, manageable society. They, too, are taught to know America as if it were Oz, not as it is but as it seems to be. They naturally believe the strength of society is in the front office. We have all been taught to think of society as a mechanical device—like an engine—which can be methodically analyzed and improved.

Contemporary social science is similar in spirit and practice to alchemy. Alchemists believed that cheap metals were perfectible, that they could be chemically transformed into precious ones. They pursued this belief with remarkable tenacity, conducting endless experiments, all of which failed, but failure never shook their faith in the fanciful premise. Some would concoct bizarre stews of beetles and crows' feet and confidently put them on to boil.

Our contemporary obsession is alchemy's cousin—the belief that society can be made more perfect—in fact, transformed—by manipulation. It is not a science at all, but a secular religion, sometimes mistakenly called liberalism.

This belief in social management is so complete that it defines progress only in terms of management's intentions, ignoring the question of whether they are achieved or not: education is what schools produce; health is what the "health delivery system" produces; economic stability is what the federal money managers create; wisdom is what comes out of universities. Thus we have little valid social thought, but instead an elaborate social mythology.

Until lately, we have "believed" in the effectiveness of certain institutionalized social procedures: prisons reform prisoners; agricultural extension stations find better ways to farm; foundations produce social inventions; police keep the peace. But none of these suppositions is true.

We have official disaster agencies that are supposed to deal with natural disasters—floods, earthquakes, tornadoes and the like. It is becoming common knowledge that these agencies are only effective in the abstract. They are practically useless when there is an actual disaster. One can imagine these official disaster fixers looking frantically for their clipboards and armbands and contingency plans while the problems are somehow being solved in other ways.

Every summer afternoon, hundreds of thousands of New Yorkers seethe and swelter as they inch along the Long

Island Expressway trying to get home. The expressway cost millions. It is a triumph of modern engineering and planning. But it doesn't work. It ruthlessly funnels traffic into a bottleneck when it clearly needs to be dispersed or replaced by mass transit. The expressway method makes a measure of sense on the Great Plains or the Arizona desert. But in a crowded city it is insane.

The cruelest alchemy of all is what the economic planners do with other people's money. Their schemes work beautifully on paper. Money, the textbooks say, is the fuel that makes business go. When the economy slows down, the government simply increases the flow of money to speed it up again. If the economy begins to go too fast—economists, thinking they are talking about something that works like an engine, say it "heats up"—the government cuts down the flow of money until business finds a safer speed. This process is called fine tuning.

But it doesn't work. Scholars who most carefully watch federal fine tuning believe it has, in practice, fueled the booms and deepened the recessions. As I write this, the final effect of this intricate, mechanical design to avoid inflation and recession has produced both. Two dozen monetary alchemists have been summoned to Washington to devise a prescription that will undo the awful consequences of their prior manipulations. For now we have inflation and stagnation at the same time. The conventional cure for either one will aggravate the other.

Economists are expressing an unfamiliar humility. "It's a lot more complicated than we economists thought," says Princeton's James Litvack. "There's a lot we don't know," says Robert Gordon, president-elect of the American Economic Association. "Find me an economist who can explain the causes of the current surge of inflation and cure it without massive unemployment and I'd like to meet him." Ironically, the situation has sharply increased the demand for economists—as the illness caused by some massive malpractice of medicine might increase the demand for doctors—and the widows and orphans most innocent of any complicity are hurt the most.

We have assumed for years that children learn to read because they are taught to read. But, writes Claremont's Professor Malcolm P. Douglass, "we have very little data to 'prove' that teaching the subject matter of reading in fact leads to proficiency in reading. We have assumed a great deal in this regard without ever seriously questioning whether cause leads to effect . . ." Our alchemistic premise is that children learn to read by first learning the alphabet and certain phonic generalizations. But this, says Professor Douglass, "is a matter that must be seriously questioned. Imagine the outcome, if you will, if speaking were taught as reading is usually taught."

Front-office America has a sociology of sorts. Unmanaged America has none. Scholars scarcely know it exists. Even the descriptive literature is hopelessly incomplete and uneven.

I first ran across this, years ago, reading a scholar's inventory of the recreational "resources" on the east shore of San Francisco Bay. The researcher had excluded practically anything that didn't happen in an official facility. Thus he carefully ignored most of what he was supposed to study. Shuffleboard at a dreary public park was recreation. A poker game was not. Nor, presumably, were bowling, pool, backyard picnics or bridge parties. He took no account of what happened in saloons or night clubs or bedrooms. And the East Bay's recreational facilities were, of course, found to be scandalously inadequate.

A loan made by a bank to General Motors becomes a part of the statistical picture of life in America. Unofficial loans made between friends do not. Thus economists are puzzled about how small businesses get started. No one knows. We know they start somehow because there are millions of them. Banks won't lend a small businessman money until he has been a success and can prove he doesn't need it. Investment bankers provide money for big existing businesses to expand. But how does a Puerto Rican immigrant start a superette in Brooklyn? I can guess that his uncles and cousins and aunts pool the money in their mattresses. But we don't know. It is not a front-office transaction, so it is ignored.

We have scarcely begun to draw the maps of the American polity. What we know about institutions is in almost direct proportion to their authoritarian character. We talk increasingly about American pluralism, but we do not know very accurately how pluralistic we are.

But more important, the social sciences rarely illuminate how America really works. If you can accept the idea that management is largely an illusion, that America only *seems* to be run by the powerful wizards in the front office, what remains to be understood is its true metabolism.

There has lately sprung up a new breed of psychologists whose work is of a radically different character from that of their predecessors. Abraham Maslow, now dead at fifty-two, was the best of them, and, I think, the most fully aware of what he was up to. This new "school" of psychology has no accepted label. It is now most often called "humanistic" psychology, but I hope that in time a better term will come into use.

Maslow's contention, as I understand it, was that most traditional psychological thought and practice had a pathological bias. Psychologists studied neuroses and psychoses—misfunctioning—and then devised clinical methods to repair them. Maslow began simply with a different emphasis or point of departure, as one can choose to say either that a glass is half full or half empty. He chose to study not mental disease, but mental health—not personality weakness, but personality strength. This means—to oversimplify it—that a practitioner can choose to identify a neurosis and try to correct it or he can displace neurosis by reinforcing psychic strength. It is far too soon to assess the full impact of humanistic psychology on the theory and practice of psychotherapy, but my hunch is that it will be enormous.

Social science is subject to a limitation exactly analogous to the one Maslow perceived in psychology.

I have always found American sociology dreary and trivial. Now I am convinced that modern sociology is tragically incomplete at its best and irrelevant at its worst. Sociologists tend to focus all their attention on malfunction —on what doesn't work—and on devising new procedures to set things right. Most of them have been trying restlessly to improve the social order without really knowing how it works. This bias is evident in practically every public or private forum bent on improving society. As a result, we are depressingly aware of what is wrong with American society, but we know very little about what is right with it.

People are self-propelling, self-actualizing. They somehow arrange themselves so that the necessary work of society is done, as if, as Adam Smith would say, they were guided by invisible hands. But because we don't know exactly how these invisible processes work, we have no solid confidence in them and instead cling desperately to the discredited conviction that management makes the world go round.

# 10

# If Management Doesn't Work, What Does?

*We know what we are, but know not what we may be.*
*—Ophelia*

Several years ago, Jane Jacobs, looking out the window of her house in Greenwich Village, observed an undiscovered invisible hand at work. To me the incident was much more exciting and important than the moon walk.

Ms. Jacobs saw an eight-year-old girl below on the sidewalk. A man was treating her a little strangely. It was too soon to see clearly whether the encounter was innocent or ominous. Ms. Jacobs began to watch.

As I watched from our second-floor window, making up my mind how to intervene if it seemed advisable, I saw it was not going to be necessary. From the butcher shop beneath the tenement had emerged the woman who, with her husband, runs the shop. She was standing within earshot of the man, her arms folded and a look of determination on her face. Joe Cornacchia, who with his sons-in-law keeps the delicatessen, emerged at about the same moment and stood solidly to the other side. Several heads poked out of the tenement windows above, one was withdrawn quickly and its owner reappeared a moment later in the doorway behind the man. Two men from the bar next to the butcher shop came to the doorway and waited. On my side of the street, I saw that the locksmith, the first man and the laundry proprietor had all come out of their shops and that the scene was also being surveyed from a number of windows besides ours. That man didn't know it, but he was surrounded.

Ms. Jacobs' conclusion:

The public peace . . . of cities is not kept primarily by the police, necessary as police are. It is kept primarily by an intricate, almost unconscious, network of voluntary controls and standards among the people themselves, and enforced by the people themselves.

Dominique, an ex-photographer with a one-word name, is head of the security committee of a block association on West 90th Street in New York City. "You can't buy security," he says. "Security is the result of the social fabric. Security begins when you see someone on the block being attacked and you yell or throw a shoe . . . Security is caring for your neighbors."

So the peace is kept in part by an invisible hand, officially unknown and undiscovered, which Jane Jacobs saw working outside her study window. There are surely hundreds more such processes, but we know about only a few.

In disasters, official agencies often fail, but invisible hands direct and coordinate the work of various unofficial specialists—firemen, policemen, physicians, nurses, priests, morticians and utility workers.

Most big organizations have elaborate and expensive

"official" communications programs. They also have an unofficial grapevine. Keith Davis, an Arizona State management professor, has found that the grapevine works better and faster. In fact, Davis says, "organizations would perish if they did not have a grapevine to fill the gaps existing in the formal communication system."

Systematic studies of positive social processes—invisible hands—are surprisingly rare, but the few which have been undertaken have produced solid, useful information.

In 1955 Harvard sociologist Carle C. Zimmerman and Lucius F. Cervantes compared successful low-income families with less successful ones. They used as their principal indicator of success the ability of families to keep their children in school past the compulsory age. They studied more than fifty thousand families, some rural, but most in inner cities. They isolated the successful families. They found that families succeeded when they were able to surround themselves with a protective network of close friend-families with highly similar values. The researchers called this phenomenon a kind of "natural social psychiatry." It was not contrived. It was, they said, a useful "social invention" which families discovered and used unconsciously as they sought to adapt to the disruptive circumstances of urban life.

At about the same time, Professor John Jewkes and two research associates studied the process of invention in much the same way. They did not accept the conventional wisdom that invention necessarily came from large research installations established to invent things. They studied successful invention without any institutional prejudice. Their study demolished the accepted proposition that the day of the lone inventor had passed. Jewkes found that invention had much more to do with attitude and atmosphere than with organization, that overorganization could thwart inventiveness.

In 1972 Dougal Robertson, his wife, three young boys and a young man they had picked up in Panama were traveling around the world in the Robertsons' yacht *Lucette*. On June 15, two hundred miles west of the Galapagos Islands, the *Lucette* was attacked by killer whales. It sank in less than a minute. The Robertson party made their way toward Central America in a rubber raft—which soon sank—and a tiny fiber-glass dinghy. Thirty-eight days later, when they were picked up by a Japanese fishing vessel, they were all in reasonably good health and only a little off course, having traveled 750 miles without charts or instruments.

Robertson's *Survive the Savage Sea* is his story of that experience and his analysis of how they made it. The manuals and most of the official survival equipment they found in the raft were nearly useless. Instruction books, he writes, "are great morale boosters, causing castaways to fall about with laughing. . . . The successful castaway will devise means to survive which no textbook can prescribe for him.

"The spirit of comradeship is a far more important factor in survival than any imposed discipline," Robertson continues. "The system of self-rationing we used for saving water was much more successful than imposed rationing could have been."

The Robertson family's survival was *technically* impossible—it could not have been managed. But they survived on unexpected reserves of determination and resourcefulness and love. They survived as if they were guided by an invisible hand.

These glimpses of unmanaged invisible processes begin

to form a kind of pattern. They reveal the elemental error of management: management must exclude and ignore the very human qualities a society most needs to stay alive. Because these qualities are not subject to precise and permanent definition, they are beyond management. You can command a man to turn a nut on an assembly line, but you cannot command him to be creative or concerned or resourceful.

It has become apparent that a society's most important quality is an ability to adapt—to change and grow.

Jane Jacobs has carefully studied the metabolism of cities. She finds that when cities deliberately or accidentally shut off the capacity for innovation, they begin to die. Efficiency, in the sense of the rehearsed repetition of established procedures, is the end of growth and the beginning of death.

Management reveres efficiency. But efficiency alone doesn't make a society keep working. What is needed is agility and adaptability.

A growing society looks messy. There is trial and error, growing and groping, trying and retrenching. A dying society, on the other hand, can look very orderly. Archaeologist Stuart Piggott writes that Mohenjo-daro and Harappā, twin capitals in an ancient Indus empire, worked with a "terrible efficiency." They produced gigantic quantities of bricks and stone weights. They produced so many identical pottery cups, Piggott thinks it may have been the custom to drink once from a cup and then break it. But these twin cities somehow lost their capacity to adapt. And in time they died.

But adaptability cannot be contrived. It is achieved in society in somewhat the same way nature achieves it.

Mutations—innovations—occur in a completely random and unpredictable way. If they are useful, they survive. If they aren't, they disappear. The new biologists are just beginning to sense the enormous flowing intricacy of this process.

Nigel Calder writes: "The strategies that populations of living things unknowingly adopt, to make the most of the genes that chance has dealt them, are very like the activities of skillful [game] players." The sickle cell anemia trait first appeared, for example, in Africa. There it is useful because it creates resistance to malaria—and it survived. The sickle cell trait is useless and destructive in America, where malaria is not a problem. And now scientists observe that the trait is steadily disappearing.

If nature were "managed," this selection process would have been cut off as soon as a reasonably workable animal or plant appeared. The multiple groping necessary for growth would have been shut off. And the natural world, having managed away its capacity to adapt, would have died.

Societies need a rich flow of innovation for growth. And as in nature, the source of innovation is often understandable in retrospect but entirely unpredictable.

John Jewkes comments on the spreading superstition that innovation can be deliberately manufactured: "The underlying principle, rarely formulated precisely, but ever present, has been that originality can be organized; that . . . mass production will produce originality just as it can produce sausages." The reality is, Jewkes continues, that "crucial discoveries . . . may spring up at practically any point and at any time."

The ball-point pen was conceived by a sculptor. Two musicians discovered the Kodachrome process. A friend of mine worked out a way to print Braille so blind people didn't have to read it backward—he was a screenwriter. Alexander Fleming discovered penicillin accidentally when one of his cultures was contaminated. A graphic artist discovered the process that became xerography. The idea for the safety razor occurred to a young traveling salesman one morning while he was shaving. Then it took many anxious months to figure out how razors could be produced in quantity. "If I had been technically trained," said King Gillette, "I would have quit." The zipper was invented by a mechanical engineer in 1891. Clothing manufacturers steadfastly refused to use it until 1923, when B. F. Goodrich finally put zippers on galoshes.

Originality simply cannot be managed. But originality is what keeps societies alive.

# 11

# The Invisible Hand Reconsidered

> . . . the best social order is not susceptible to being . . .
> scientifically constructed.
> —Alexander Solzhenitsyn

The practical business of society seems to need management. It is fairly easy to see how natural selection works in nature. Innovations that work survive and flourish. Innovations that are impractical for one reason or another simply fade away. But the selection process in society is not so clear. The idea of letting human diversity flourish without discipline seems, on the face of it, insane.

How can the efforts of the millions of entities that make up American society add up to a national overall result unless they are managed?

How can we be sure that this chaotic array of institutions will produce the right things at the right place at the right time? How can we know that we will not produce too many shoes and not enough socks? How can we be sure that urgent tasks will not be left undone, that the public business will be attended to unevenly? We can imagine practically everybody choosing to make sandals in storefront shops and nobody choosing to empty bedpans. We can imagine houses being built with no streets to connect them.

The main problem of a society is the business of matching and rematching its enormously diffuse and changing resources to an immense, ever-changing and complex agenda of wants and needs.

Logically, the only way to solve this problem is to manage it, to communicate "needs" to some central place which can then methodically assign tasks to acting entities, then watch to be sure these assignments are fulfilled, and somehow discipline those who fail to perform. This is plausible, but it doesn't work.

What does work is, regrettably, implausible. The activities of many of our businesses are coordinated without management—by an "invisible hand" which Adam Smith discovered and analyzed in *The Wealth of Nations*. Businesses manage the people who work for them—often ruthlessly. But many businesses are not themselves managed. Their activities are harmonized by a kind of natural selection.

We usually call this economic process the "free enterprise system," or the "profit system." But these labels distort the reality. It is not a system. It is—quite the opposite—the absence of a system, a nonsystem. It is neither managed nor planned. The Secretary of Commerce is in no sense in charge of it. It works as if it were "run" by a wonderfully keen intelligence with a marvelously enlightened comprehension of human psychology. It is in fact not run by anybody.

Businessmen do not, on the whole, believe in free

enterprise. They are fervid supporters of the comfortable half of the free enterprise ideal, the part which says business should be free of regulation.

But I have never met a businessman who liked competition and who would not evade its discipline if he possibly could. "The only time a man loses his dislike for monopoly," writes the *Wall Street Journal's* George Shea, "is when he has a chance of forming one."

Most American businesses have found shelter from competition in one way or another.

I used to escape from NAM to drink coffee at the drugstore across the street, and listen for a while to the Brooklyn counterman's continuous monologue on the state of the nation. He was, among other things, fiercely antibusiness. He was convinced, for example, that all canned foods were produced by a single giant combine, but that a variety of labels were arbitrarily affixed to various products to create the illusion of competition where none really existed.

At the time, we at NAM were, as usual, laboring to "get the business message to the grass roots," but when I listened to the counterman, it became clear that this great educational program had not yet reached across the street.

This gave me pause. I had thoughtlessly assumed for years that businessmen favored free enterprise, and were its natural spokesmen. But when I thought about it more carefully, I realized that the doctrine American businessmen proclaim is selective and corrupt and understandably unconvincing. As I reread the history of American business in this light, I found that the American business tradition is not a free enterprise tradition, but simply a blind "go-getter" tradition. Businessmen have never hesitated for a moment to conspire with government officials to shelter themselves from the harsher half of the free enterprise gospel. The most determined booster of free enterprise I ever knew was a businessman who collected millions every year for not farming land he owned in Nebraska. The Dodge brothers sued Henry Ford successfully because he paid his workers too much and sold his cars for too little.

The forms of insulation from the competitive selection process are as varied as business itself. The broadcast network monopoly is fiercely defended by the Federal Communications Commission; privileges worth billions are passed out like chewing gum samples. Automobile manufacturers prosper from billion-dollar highway subsidies. Milk producers have price supports; oil producers have depletion allowances. Supermarkets function in a protected atmosphere created by city ordinances banning pushcart peddlers.

The technical basis for AT&T's "natural" monopoly has all but disappeared, but the company fights ferociously for its monopoly rights.

A pure example of free enterprise is as rare as the whooping crane. Moonshiners, maybe. Even prostitution is a regulated monopoly in Nevada. The doctors absolutely control entry into the practice of medicine and then complain about the shortage of doctors.

At NAM, certain subjects, such as tariffs, were unmentionable. A determined minority of the membership depended on the insulation tariffs provided for their prosperity.

Public policy is increasingly anticompetitive. Tax policy makes it possible for giant companies to buy up little ones at about half price.

But the *reality* of free enterprise, unpopular as it is

among businessmen, is, when you can find it, a valid model of a complex social process that works without conscious management. The daily task the process accomplishes, when it is allowed to work, is to perceive millions of diverse needs and translate them into signals in a language that everybody understands, so that all the nation's resources can arrange and rearrange themselves automatically.

The economic process is usually explained in terms of profit motivation and competitive discipline, so we get the impression that the process communicates instructions like "Work hard and don't waste anything." But Adam Smith's invisible hand does much more than stimulate effort and penalize waste. It works as a master arranger or harmonizer of diverse human effort and it works without control. The invisible hand that coordinates the economic process holds neither a carrot nor a stick. It is a signaling hand, important mainly for the kind of directions it provides and the way it communicates them.

I think I began to understand the nature of the economic process about ten years ago when John Jewkes patiently retold to me an analogy which he attributed to Edwin Cannan:

Suppose you have a pile of rocks, of widely different shapes and sizes, and a bag. The problem is to arrange the rocks in the bag so that they use up the least possible amount of space. There are two ways you could go about it. You could, using elaborate instruments, measure each rock in all its dimensions. (I am told that for a knobby, irregular rock, this definition alone would occupy several pages); then you could painstakingly calculate how much space would be displaced by all the possible combinations of the rocks, and, having discovered the optimum plan, you could arrange the rocks, one at a time, according to it. Or: you could shake the bag

Now, the analogy conveys only a tiny fraction of the complexity involved in arranging and rearranging the incomprehensible diversity of people and institutions that make up a modern society. Rocks have only three dimensions, and all are measurable. Human beings have at least hundreds, most of which are beyond measurement.

To make matters worse—or better—these human qualities are literally changing all the time. And so are their objectives. The purposes of the arrangement—unlike mere space-saving—are incomprehensibly complex and they too change every instant.

The free economic process shows each participant how to find his own way into a useful position in the larger mosaic. It is as if each rock knew the way to its place and moved there, as when the bag is shaken, without being told. The way this happens in practice is illuminated by the concept of feedback, as applied to computers and guidance systems.

Suppose the problem is to hit a haystack with a mortar. The haystack is over a hill out of sight. If there is no way to find out whether you hit the haystack or not, there is no feedback. You can shoot the mortar endlessly, telling yourself that the more shells you fire the greater the likelihood you will hit the haystack. This method succeeds only by accident, and wastes a lot of ammunition. (Obviously, under these circumstances, the biggest liar is more likely to rise in the gun crew than is the best gunner.)

Now, if you can put a scout in a tree where he can see the haystack, you can introduce a measure of feedback into the proceedings. You fire the mortar; the scout observes the accuracy of the shot and communicates his findings to you.

And, obviously, the usefulness of the feedback depends on its precision. If the observer simply laughs hysterically, it is not helpful. "Jesus, Charley, that wasn't even close," is not as helpful as, "A little to the left and a little lower," which is not as helpful as, "Left 7 units and down 2 units." Instructions like these constitute a kind of feedback, and clearly, they are better than nothing. But it is soft feedback, dependent on the perception and integrity and nimbleness of the observer.

Devices exist, I'm told, which can perceive exactly how far and in what direction the mortar misses the target, and exactly how the aim of the gun must be corrected. And, most important, the device can be connected to a power source which moves the muzzle of the mortar, so that the mortar, regardless of how erratically the target moves, is automatically trained and retrained on it. Such a system, if it works perfectly, can hit a target every time, even as it moves in wholly unpredictable directions.

For feedback to work effectively, it has to have two qualities: it has to be able to give a quantity (it can't say a little to the right, it has to say exactly how much to the right), and it has to have force (it can't merely suggest that the gun move its muzzle, it has to be able to move the muzzle or activate a force which moves the muzzle). The force is necessary in a guidance system because the gun muzzle is inert. It cannot move itself.

But the actors in the economic process are self-propelling. Economic feedback reaches them in the form of unmistakable signals. Guided by these signals, people move themselves. In this way the process is self-managing. It works without authority, and it works sensibly, creating order out of potential chaos.

The crucial quality of the system is that it works

88

without conscious management. F. A. Hayek, who perhaps understands this process better than anyone else, writes eloquently about it. Discussing how the invisible hand deals with any economic problem, such as the shortage of a raw material like tin or cotton, he says:

The marvel is that . . . without an order being issued, without more than perhaps a handful of people knowing the cause, tens of thousands of people whose identity could not be ascertained by months of investigation, are made to use the material or its products more sparingly; that is, they move in the right direction. . . .

But those who clamor for "conscious direction"—and who cannot believe that anything which has evolved without design (and even without our understanding it) can solve problems which we cannot solve consciously—should remember this: the problem is precisely how to extend the utilization of resources beyond the span of the control of any one mind; and, therefore, how to dispense with the need of conscious control, how to provide inducements which will make individuals do the desirable things without anyone having to tell them what to do.

The economic process thus creates a unique, psychological atmosphere. It does much more than simply motivate people to act. It invites them to act imaginatively. It invites them to innovate, to discover new, promising ways to get things done.

B. F. Skinner has developed psychological atmospheres which cause people to behave in "desired" ways. His method, popularly known as positive reinforcement, has been widely adopted by teachers and managers, and to teach pigeons to play ping-pong. The economic process is slightly Skinnerian. It reinforces success and is comparatively gentle with failure. It doesn't rebuke or punish those who fail. It just doesn't reward them.

But the economic process really goes beyond Skinner. Its workings were greatly illuminated for me when I read about some remarkable experiments with porpoises conceived by Karen Pryor at Sea Life Park in Hawaii. She had been training sea animals for some time using conventional Skinnerian methods, which she described in *Psychology Today* with a fine clarity:

> Suppose you want to train a pilot or killer whale. You must first teach the whale that when he hears a whistle he will be given a fish. Then you decide exactly what you want the whale to do and teach him to perform by rewarding actions that come closer and closer to your goal, marking each action with a whistle blast and then a fish. If you want your whale to jump 20 feet straight up out of the water, you hold a padded stick in the water. When the whale, out of curiosity, touches the stick, you blow the whistle and feed the whale. Soon the whale will touch the stick eagerly each time he sees it. Now you hold the stick just out of the water; the whale touches it and gets his fish. Gradually you raise the stick higher and higher. In a few days the whale will jump 20 feet to earn his fish—and will jump at the sight of the stick held in the air. This process is called shaping.

And this is, at least in part, the psychological atmosphere the economic process creates. It is possible to imagine Adam Smith writing: "Suppose you want to train a businessman. You must first teach the businessman that . . ." And so forth.

But then came Karen Pryor's delicious post-Skinnerian discovery. She and her crew give daily public demonstrations of their teaching methods. One of the things they demonstrate at these shows is the process described above, the "shaping" of a new "behavior." But of course they can't show how porpoises learn by putting them through paces they already know. It has to be something new. So, Ms. Pryor writes, "We adopted a new rule: we would only reward those actions that had not been rewarded before." The results were astonishing. "Within a few days we had used up all the normal casual actions of a porpoise. Then Malia [the female porpoise they used in these demonstrations] began doing serial flips, gliding with her tail out of water and skidding on the tank floor. . . . *Some of Malia's spontaneous stunts were so unusual that the trainers couldn't imagine achieving them with the shaping system.*"

And that is what the economic process does. It invites and rewards behavior that can exceed the imagination. It is open-ended. No shaping system could have produced Henry Ford. No shaping system could produce another Henry Ford. The economic process is *not* a shaping system. It is the opposite. That is why the free economic process is superproductive. It has much less to do with the nature of the incentives it provides—money or mackerel or medals—than with the *kind* of behavior it "chooses" to reward.

Karen Pryor went on more methodically to induce *creative* behavior in porpoises. The results were extraordinary. In time, she quit the experiment because the porpoises' acrobatics "had become so complex that they exceeded the ability of observers to describe them."

Viewed this way, the workings of the economic process suggest a way to run society without authority. Instructions must be expressed precisely and in terms which specify a desired *result* instead of a known procedure or behavior.

# Part IV
# De-Managing Organizations

# 12

# Internalizing the Invisible Hand

If the boss calls, get his name.
—A middle manager at General Electric

Businessmen tend to accept the Jeffersonian proposition that governments govern best when they govern least. But they reject its corollary: that companies manage best when they manage least.

Businessmen believe that they should be free of management by government authorities, that business should operate in a free atmosphere, but what happens inside business is usually another matter altogether. People who work for businesses aren't treated the way businessmen themselves instinctively want to be treated. They are told when to come to work, and often what to wear. They are guided by endless manuals. Their curiosity is stifled, their humanity diminished. And as soon as their performance is subject to someone else's judgment, they become politicized. Their success is dependent on pressure and popularity.

Business executives tend to believe that management works and that they are good at it. They are wrong on both counts.

Elaborate bodies of material called management science are packaged and taught to youngsters. But if you look at this science closely, it is largely self-contradictory, and no more scientific than the plausible sure-fire systems of race-track touts.

One of Milton Friedman's hobbies is collecting contradictory folk wisdom. He believes that for every absolute expressed in a folk saying like "He who hesitates is lost," there is an equally revered opposite like "Haste makes waste." This tends to be true of management theory. There is a school of thought, for example, that says business decisions should be made quickly: Do it now. But I understand that Du Pont executives are encouraged to delay decisions as long as possible, on the plausible grounds that more facts will come to the surface as time passes.

And probably the most awful examples of nonsense in print are the books of successful businessmen who try to explain their successes retrospectively. Clement Stone believes he succeeded because of his "positive mental attitude" and seems puzzled why more people don't just grin and get rich.

Businessmen appear to run their businesses as the Wizard appeared to run Oz. They go through the motions of management and assume that they are causal. But the truth is that businesses largely run themselves. For one thing, the most crucial "management" decisions are made *for* business managers and are wholly beyond their control.

A businessman, whether he knows it or not, operates like a mouse in a maze. If he moves very far in the wrong direction, he is "shocked" by declining sales or profits. He changes his course and runs in some new direction. If he is positively reinforced by rising sales and profits, he keeps running, until new signals tell him to try still another direction. The businessman doesn't control the shape of the maze. He simply finds his way through it by trial and error.

Businessmen like to think of themselves as great planners. But far more business plans fail than succeed. The contrary illusion is created because we hear a lot about the plans that worked and next to nothing about the ones that didn't.

One company I know well spent something over $50 million developing a new product, including more than a million just for market research. Its plans were exhaustive, incorporating literally hundreds of variables, projected years in advance to the third decimal place. When it launched the product, after three years of preparation, nobody would buy it. The plan was worthless.

Had the company succeeded—and there was no sure way to tell it wouldn't—its officers would have been lecturing on long-range planning at the Harvard Business School. As it is, they are looking for work.

I have known a lot of businessmen at one time or another. I have admired many of them for their industriousness and their nerve. But the quality common to the most successful of them was not some gift for management, but a kind of cracker realism that caused them to swallow their losses promptly and change course when market forces outside their control signaled that it was time for a change.

But when they have a choice, businessmen tend to believe in the myth of management as devoutly as any bishop in the Catholic hierarchy, if not more so.

Whenever companies are somehow sheltered from the economic weather and are free to make unchecked decisions, as in the case of protected monopolies like AT&T or Con Edison, they become manifestly inefficient, as anyone who has ever dealt with either of these monstrosities will cheerfully testify.

But at least in good times, we tend to attribute magical management skills to businessmen. Politicians recruit them into government positions, expecting marvelous results. I have seen many of these transplants at close range in Washington. If anything, they get rather worse results than career bureaucrats.

Consider Robert McNamara and his "whiz kids." He added the rhetoric of efficiency to the operation of the Defense Department, but the cost of maintaining the military establishment rose enormously during his tenure. He may well have been the most irresponsible defense chief in the short history of that office.

Furloughed businessmen in government tend to lead government into new pastures of profligacy because their hyperactivity is unchecked by market necessity and because Congress tends to be less critical of them. Roy Ash's diligent efforts to make government work better were a flop. Businessmen were deeply involved in the Nixon administration's program to promote Black capitalism. It has failed utterly. George Romney's experience as head of American Motors did not prevent him from producing some of the biggest bloopers in the history of big government—as, for instance, Operation Breakthrough.

One of the nation's most widely respected practical psychologists, Fred E. Fiedler of the University of Washington, has concluded after countless careful studies that management training doesn't work. "American business, industry and government," he writes in *Psychology Today*, "have poured billions of dollars into training programs that try to teach managers how to make their organizations more effective. This enormous investment has produced little measurable return. . . . No one has established a consistent, direct correlation between the amount or type of a leader's training and the performance of the group he leads."

Fieldler recently studied 171 post office managers and supervisors. Some had had years of training; some had had none. There was no difference in their performance. Management cannot be a science. It cannot be taught. People are not, essentially, manageable. But business persists in trying to manage them anyway.

Consider the work of a secretary to an executive in a conventional office. She is told exactly when to come to work and when she can leave. She is told when she can go to the bathroom and for how long. Management follows her into the ladies' room, where she is admonished not to put Kotex in the toilet, not to splash the mirror, and to smile so the world will smile with her.

She has an excruciatingly detailed manual of office procedures in her bottom drawer. She knows that she must "please" her "boss." But she can never be sure how. She must pretend to like him if she hates his guts. She must agree with him when she thinks he is dead wrong. She must play horrid political games with him. She lives in fear of offending him or misjudging his moods. She must endure his adolescent flirtations. She must worry about whether the way she dresses is "acceptable." Her security is subject to whims beyond her knowledge and control. She functions in that awful twilight between a fully human life and the life of a trained chimpanzee. She is often called a "girl" as Black men were once called "boy." She is trapped by her boss's conception of her. She cannot go beyond it. She is a "secretary."

The organization that employs such a woman cheats itself of the difference between her full potential and their limiting conception of her.

Supervisors constantly complain about their problems with people: "All my problems are people problems." An engineer doesn't feel thwarted because steel is heavy or granite hard. But the work of a human engineer is based on an engineeringlike assumption that people "should" be wholly tractable. So the human manager feels betrayed when people don't act like things. Management specialist Richard T. Johnson writes, "We've done very well coping with the inanimate elements of management. But a shocking number of American managers are really inept in dealing with people."

As businessmen learn to promulgate free enterprise inside their businesses I think much of the people's apparent animosity to the free market will dissolve.

"Do not bend, mutilate or fold," the antibusiness battle cry of the humanist youngsters, is not an anti-enterprise sentiment. It is an anti-authoritarian sentiment. When people get fed up with business and "drop out," they do not necessarily disappear. Most of them start little businesses on the Bleecker Streets of the country. They become enterprisers, recognizing, at least practically if not intellectually, that the free market provides the emancipating atmosphere they long to live in. One of them, Carl Tendler, after fourteen years as an aerospace engineer, opened an antique shop in my neighborhood. "I'm doing about as well as I would had I stuck to a management-type job," he says, "but I don't have all the headaches and red tape to put up with. I make all the decisions. I'm in total control."

Carl and thousands of others, reports *The New York Times,* have struck out on their own to cure the "Sunday evening syndrome"—"the attacks of nervous anxiety and depression that were brought on by the thought of the five-day office routine that loomed ahead."

Businessmen, like all of us, tend to get confused about the problem management exists to solve. The problem is not to get people to do what they are told, but to do what they are not told, or even what they can't be told.

It seems to me that one of the most marvelous devices ever conceived for the constructive coordination of human energy is the taximeter. Every day in New York City a miraculous, flowing arrangement and rearrangement of people and vehicles takes place. Hundreds of thousands of people, with as many unknowable destinations, connect with the thousands of cabs cruising the city in search of fares. A computer could never solve the problem the cab "system" solves unconsciously every day. Too many of the elements are unknowable, and they change too fast. Of course there are rush-hour delays and mistakes. But experienced fares know where to look for cabs. The cabs tend, by dispatching themselves, to flow to wherever they are most needed. And this incomprehensibly complex system is not managed. It manages itself. And the device that makes this automaticity possible is the taximeter.

The fleet owner gives the driver one simple instruction: to come back with $60 or more on his "clock." He needs no further supervision. He is not told where to go. Leaving

aside radio dispatching, which accounts for only a tiny fraction of New York's daily payload, New York cabs are self-dispatching.

The cabbie is not given a manual. He is not watched or guided. He is not told how to dress or how to "behave." He is free not of work but of politicized work.

One result, which strikes any cab rider instantly, is the staggering diversity of human eccentricity the system employs. Some drivers wear a kind of chauffeur's uniform. Some wear T-shirts. Some dress like bank clerks, others wear bizarre costumes. In the summer, some drive in swimsuits. Some are sweet and some are surly. Some share Archie Bunker's world view; some are latter-day Wobblies. Some talk interminably, some only grunt once and drive in silence. But all this dissonance is harmonized into a rational result by the taximeters.

Most of the fleet owners who "manage" cabbies have never heard of Harvard Business School. They have never read a book about management. Some of them, I'm told, can hardly read at all. But they are unconsciously employing the most sophisticated and far-sighted management method of all—they manage by not managing, by treating each person as a microcosm of the larger economic process. They provide an unmistakable framework in which employees can manage themselves.

And it works.

Management which manages by specifying *behavior* is dehumanizing and inefficient. Management which manages by specifying *results* is emancipating. It opens to all the possibility of inventiveness and resourcefulness. It is a way of depoliticizing the management process. It is highly productive, because it tends to release the full potential of people, rather than some predetermined and necessarily deformed fraction of that potential.

Business executives do have an indispensable role to play. They must read the signals of the market most carefully, decide what products their firm will produce, and assemble the resources that are necessary to produce those products.

But they perform best when they do not presume to manage the people they assemble. It is now becoming clear that businesses work better when businessmen learn that people are unmanageable, and when they provide not supervision but the same kind of working atmosphere in which they themselves work.

Bob Townsend, once the successful maverick president of Avis, has since written a light-hearted book about management called *Up the Organization*. Its essential message is very clear. Townsend was successful because he didn't try to run Avis. He knew he couldn't, so he let it run itself. Businessmen function best when they see their function as guidance, when they see themselves as allocators of responsibility, and not as managers.

Business couldn't work without accounting. Double-entry bookkeeping, conceived centuries ago by a forgotten Catholic priest, probably had much more to do with the blossoming of business than any other single innovation. It is essentially a way of internalizing market information, of hypothetically pricing things which really have no price because they are not traded. When accounting is carried to its ultimate application, when *every employee* is a hypothetical profit center, then everyone can function exactly as the boss himself functions. Then the apparent need for management will disappear.

The necessity to internalize the messages of the market, and substitute them for outworn authoritarian methods, has become a discernible trend in the accounting profession. It is called "responsibility accounting." One of its pioneers, M. J. Gordon, professor of business administration at the University of Rochester, wrote ten years ago in the *N.A.A. Bulletin*:

Responsibility accounting . . . represents the design and employment of the accounting system for the purpose of introducing market relations as a supplement—some would say substitute°— for authority relations in the administration of an organization . . . The problem was obvious: bureaucracy and/or chaos in a firm that had grown too large for top management to manage by direct supervision and decision. The solution appeared no less obvious: carry the direction, information and motivation provided by a profit figure down to the lower levels of management.

More and more companies are experimenting with demanagement, either for individual employees or for small groups of employees. One such experiment is in a General Foods Gaines dog-food plant in Topeka. The work force is broken down into teams of ten, each with a group leader. The leader presents goals. The workers decide together how the goals shall be reached. The smell of authority has largely disappeared. Workers can take any parking space in the lot outside the plant. None are reserved for "management." There are no time clocks to punch, no rigid lunch hours to keep in segregation.

It works. Absenteeism and turnover at the Gaines plant are low. Productivity is a third higher than in comparable "managed" plants.

° I would.

"Our assumption," says Edward Dulworth, who arranged the experiment, "was that people are concerned, trustworthy and will respond to responsibility. Our aim was to create an environment that would let them use these qualities. The guts of the thing is that each man has autonomy to decide how we're going to do things." The key word is "how." "I really feel more like a human being than a worker," Andy Dodge, one of the Gaines workers told *Newsweek*.

IBM has reorganized a typewriter assembly plant in Amsterdam according to the same principle. Before the reform, seventy workers worked on each of two two-hundred-meter assembly lines. Each worker worked for three minutes on each passing typewriter. Now there are nine mini-lines, with about twenty workers assigned to each. The assemblers make many of the "how" decisions—production, engineering, quality control and materials handling. Absenteeism and turnover rates are down dramatically. Production dropped at first after the changeover and then rose steadily. In two years it was up 46 percent.

Polaroid, Texas Instruments, General Electric—even Ford and Chrysler—are experimenting with demanagement. The Department of Health, Education and Welfare believes that maybe three thousand people work in demanaged atmospheres.

Indiana Bell used to assemble its phone books in twenty-one supersimplified steps performed by twenty-one separate workers. Now each clerk assembles an entire book. This simple reform cut turnover rates in half.

Conventional managers are understandably uneasy. Michael Beer, a new-breed organization man at Corning Glass, says established managers often tell him that he "doesn't know a damn thing about management." And this, of course, is true. He knows instead how to get results without management. At Corning's Medford plant, demanagement increased production twenty percent and doubled efficiency.

If this tendency to demanage continues, the distasteful trappings of authority—the executive men's room, pretentious titles and the rest—will in time disappear. Some people, according to ability and inclination, will have more responsibility than others. But everyone will have essentially the same *kind* of responsibility. A new kind of elemental equality will prevail. A company will become an association of equal specialists. Some will specialize in steering the company. Others will specialize in translating these decisions into quantified guidelines for the rest. But no one will boss anybody else. Authority, in the sense we now know it, will disappear.

If businesses decide to demanage, or if workers insist on it—or both—productivity will multiply. The capacities of people will be more fully engaged in the work process. The possible sources of innovation will multiply. It is absolutely predictable that the rate of innovation and the rate at which proven innovations are universally adopted will both quicken.

There will be some welcome side effects if firms are demanaged. The source of much tension and resentment will disappear along with the depoliticization of internal corporate affairs. Communication will be more open and less pretentious. Employees will be free of the emptiness of functioning subhumanly.

I may live to see an office manual displayed at the Smithsonian along with the mummy cases and chastity belts, as a weird artifact of a bygone era.

Where is the pressure to de-manage coming from? Not, I think, from the front office.

Unmanaged America is becoming more conscious of itself and its possibilities. People are beginning to realize that they do not have to be treated like furniture to make the world work. They are quietly insisting on working atmospheres that are fit for human habitation. Andy Dodge at the Gaines plant in Topeka was vaguely uncomfortable all his life; now he finally "feels like a human being."

This revolution° in self-consciousness—begun by Blacks, the most oppressed, and then greatly extended by women—is now beginning to reach the Andy Dodges of the world. A hunch—that people do best when their human qualities are not shut off—is blossoming into a conscious conviction.

Where are the leaders, the press wants to know? This kind of revolt needs no leadership—it has outgrown leadership.

What is happening is the beginning of what could become a mass emancipation, and the great emancipators are the people themselves. It may be irreversible. "After this," says Andy Dodge, "there is no way you could get me to go back into regular employment."

But unless we leave off mismanaging the public business, Andy Dodge may not have any job at all.

---

° These modern movements—the civil rights movement, the women's movement —were themselves distinctly unmanaged. Their leaders did not impose rigid structures or procedures on the participants. Coordinated only by their common concerns, the Blacks, the women, and the students were largely on their own. Their informal networks looked messy, but they were tremendously effective.

## Part V

# De-Managing the Public Business

# 13

# Institutional Identity

Organizations have personalities.

—Harry Levinson

The nation is misusing its institutions in much the same way that managed organizations are misusing people: an authoritarian office manager acts on the basis of demeaning, irrational prejudices about the people he tries to manage, and thus he assigns elaborate procedures to them, instead of prescribing results. Our government bodies, and most of all the federal government, act on arcane and irrational superstitions about the capacities of the nation's institutions. And it then compounds the error by assigning procedures to them.

But here too, if you look for them, there are signs of change. There are some promising experiments here and there in a kind of taximeter government.

An awareness of institutional identity becomes a cru-cial element in the de-management of society—just as a heightened sense of individual identity is the principal propellant of change within organizations. There are signs that a search for institutional identity is at least beginning.

Here are some examples drawn from my own experience.

The National Association of Manufacturers is an organization I know rather well. I worked as its executive vice-president for nearly three years. I had watched it casually for years before the president hired me, and I have kept an eye on it since I left five years ago.

The NAM is a lot of things. It is an anachronism. It is a joke. It is a terror-stricken organization. But most of all, I think, it is a paper tiger. It is a classic case of an organization with a mistaken sense of identity. NAM is not, of course, alone. Thousands of American organizations are just now struggling to correct serious misconceptions about themselves. Such organizations, I have found, have a neurotic supersensitivity to public opinion. Their internal politics are usually ferocious. They are guilt-ridden. They reorganize every Tuesday, to create the illusion of vitality where there is no real vitality. They spend a disproportionate amount of energy merely maintaining their constituencies.°

It seems to me that NAM's neurosis is simple and elemental. It lives with the illusion that it is a powerful organization. It is an understandable mistake. The press chooses to treat NAM as a powerful organization. I thought

° The parallels to an individual with a faulty sense of identity are unmistakable. Such a person is neurotically concerned about what people think of him. He is at war with himself. He is guilt-ridden. He is forever restlessly rearranging his life. He spends most of his energy keeping his internal balance, and has very little left over to do anything.

it was powerful when I joined it. When I attended various ritual events around the country, and was introduced as the executive vice-president of the National Association of Manufacturers, people would gasp and I could imagine some of them trembling a little.

But the power of NAM is a myth. The facts are these.

There was a time, just before World War I, when the power of NAM was in fact awesome. It was the high noon of the era of big manufacturing, and the big manufacturers were powerful. Most of them belonged to NAM. To leave nothing to chance, NAM decided what Congress should do in advance. NAM had fashioned its committee structure after the committee structure of Congress. The members divided themselves up among these committees and decided what laws should be passed. Their annual meeting, at which the recommendations of these shadow Congressional committees were considered by representatives of all the members, was unabashedly called the Congress of American Industry. This mini-Congress was almost as important as Congress itself. It was held at the Waldorf Astoria Hotel in the late fall, a couple of months before the U.S. Congress convened after the turn of the year. In those days, a member of the real Congress ignored at his peril the recommendations of the Congress of American Industry. The law of the land was often written at the Waldorf.

Times have changed. NAM now has a motley membership of about twelve thousand of the hundreds of thousands of commercial organizations eligible to join. It spends about $6 million a year—less, for instance, than Planned Parenthood or a suburban department store. Its influence with Congress is a little less than zero. NAM's main output during the year are a few additions or amendments to a kind of bible called *Industry Believes*. This title is itself excessive. It constitutes the "beliefs" of a sometimes tiny majority of the tiny fraction of members of NAM who are active in their tedious deliberations, and who in fact "represent" only a small misshapen fraction of industry. In the second place, *Industry Believes* is unreadable. In the third place, the deliberation machinery is so clumsy that NAM often decides what industry believes after Congress has acted. And in the fourth place, Congress long ago left off caring what NAM believes.

Nevertheless, NAM moves in the world with all the pomp of a superpower. It still meets solemnly in the Grand Ballroom of the Waldorf Astoria in November with the captains of industry arranged in endless tiers of what must be the largest dais in the world, the whiskey bottles concealed from the press photographers under gleaming linen tablecloths.

NAM could be of some use to its members and to the world. But not when it thinks of itself as powerful when in fact it has no power. NAM is even sadder than organizations corrupted by power. NAM is corrupted by a mistaken sense of power.

But some businessmen are beginning to develop a brighter vision of the natural mission of business associations. William C. Stolk, as chairman of the Committee of Economic Development, speaks most clearly and sensibly about it.

Corporate social action, Stolk points out, is still largely a torrent of pious talk. There is a reason. In the market, for better or for worse, nice corporations finish last. A corporation that spends heavily to abate pollution compromises its commercial position. It isn't accidental that the most public-spirited companies are found in the least competitive industries. Thus, irresponsibility sets the pace. "The result," says Stolk, "is that business generally proceeds by the lowest common denominator of industry action—or inaction. Government then has to take over. . . . Business pays the bill, which is almost always higher than if industry had done the job in the first place. . . .

"This is self-defeating. And it isn't too difficult to find a better way. The machinery is already in place—industry or trade associations. What we have to do is turn them around: convert them from rear-guard defenders of the status quo into instrumentalities for collective industry action in the public interest.

"The industry association is the place where corporate public business executives can bring their proposed action programs—sort out who does what—decide on a fair apportionment of the costs—and work out a detailed industry plan and time schedule for solving the problem."

I wish I had had this clear sense of the potential of business associations when I was at NAM. But it seems to me that associations will inevitably move in this direction, not, I am afraid, because their managers see the light, but because their members insist on it. A half-dozen big companies with a solid sense of purpose could, for example, turn NAM around in a fortnight.

Business firms very often have identity problems of their own which they tend to drench with public relations programs, in much the same way that an insecure woman wears too much perfume to a job interview.

There has thus been for years an obscene emphasis on corporate "image." An image-obsessed company painstakingly polls its various "publics" to find out how it is regarded. Then, more often than not, it hires a high-priced corporate cosmetologist called a public relations counselor to change the company's appearance. The superficiality of these proceedings is often appalling and the practice of public relations is sometimes not far from quackery, exploiting the insecurity of clients most cynically.*

When you see a carefully rehearsed method actor on television looking at his shoes and saying on Ford's behalf, "We listen better," you can bet that behind it is some hotshot PR man with a tattersall vest and a mess of data showing that people think Ford is unresponsive.

Industry's insecurity is, I think, rooted in some deep-seated doubts about how companies make money and even the legitimacy of profit seeking. Companies are thus tempted to keep two sets of books and two PR firms—one pair to tell Wall Street they are making a killing, and the other to tell the liberal press that their profits are in fact modest, and that, in any case, they are really more interested in social work than in making money.

But when Milton Friedman tells businessmen that they will serve the public interest best if they forget the nonsense about corporate responsibility and simply try to maximize their profits, he is giving them a dangerous fraction of the truth. It is one thing to say that trying to maximize profits is not in any sense evil, and moreover that a company cannot survive without making profits. But to escalate these sound perceptions into a point of view that says the only role of a business is to seek profits is to misread Adam Smith in the

---

* A few public relations men, like Gershon Kekst of Kekst and Company, try instead to help companies understand themselves.

same way people have read into Freud a vocational view of sex.

This limited point of view has produced a kind of corporate machismo and a breed of businessmen who swagger and boast about their single-minded focus on the "bottom line," and who consider the growing minority of big businessmen groping for a larger vision of the corporation's mission to be pantywaists.

It is perfectly true that any honorable commercial transaction between consenting adults is legitimate, that a company cannot survive without making profits, and moreover, that profit differentials are an indispensable guide to rational allocation of resources. But it does not follow that a company must view itself only as a profit-making machine. A modern corporation is a much more intricate social entity. But corporate consciousness is surprisingly low: many companies misperceive even the limited commercial aspects of their nature.

One company I worked with a couple of years ago started with nothing but the patent on an ingenious and appealing little household gadget. It sold literally millions of these humble devices, grew very rapidly and made a lot of money.

The men who ran the company began to perceive themselves as uniquely gifted managers. They began a headlong acquisition program, impatiently buying up companies that made paint, ran hotels and published magazines. All these adventures failed financially, causing the company to look more closely at its strengths and weaknesses, and a kind of panicky identity search was organized.

It was most illuminating. The success of the little gadget was indeed a lucky punch. But its appeal, studied

116

more closely, was neither frivolous nor ephemeral. It was
the accidental beginning of a new and potentially very large
industry.

Now the company is developing in a much more solid
and methodical way. It will surprise me very much if it does
not continue to grow and prosper. But it very nearly
drowned because it misunderstood itself.

"No two businesses," writes Peter Drucker, "are alike
in their distinct knowledge." General Electric is good at
starting companies, General Motors at developing companies once they have started. Neither seems to be good at the
other function. One research company Drucker describes
failed miserably on some assignments and succeeded mag-
nificently on others. The company was puzzled and shaken
until Drucker found out that it performed well with tight
deadlines and badly against loose ones.

Companies or institutions with identity problems[*]
often lack a ready vocabulary for describing themselves and
the markets they serve. This often leads them to accept the
labels their detractors coin, and thus they get stuck with
abusive designations. The overall enterprise process, for
example, is most often called capitalism, a term Karl Marx
was the first to use and which he meant as an insult.

More recently, "conglomerate" companies have accepted a pejorative designation coined by a skeptical
observer, but such companies now use the term to identify
themselves, just as one of my sixth-grade classmates came to
call himself "Stinky."

[*] Regrettably, the firms who design letterheads and trademarks and logotypes have
appropriated the phrase "corporate identity" when they are really dealing with the
humbler business of corporate identification. The difference is as important as the
difference between psychoanalysts and haberdashers.

But some businesses are changing. They are gathering in consciousness-raising sessions with titles like "Corporate Social Responsibility—the Emerging Consensus." The frequency and sophistication of such gatherings is increasing perceptibly.

When one Congressman set out to catalog corporate social action projects, the result was not one volume but a shelfful. The corporation's noncommercial activities are getting more and more attention in the front office. A journal specializing in this aspect of the corporate experience is being published. Standards and guidelines are being suggested and debated. If there is a consensus, it is a very limited one. But corporations are beginning to recognize that it is short-sighted and unhealthy to ignore their capacities for public service.

Foundations are a unique and potentially very exciting part of the American polity, but probably one of the clumsiest and least fulfilling of their potential.

First of all, foundations are given to a disabling illusion of omniscience. I worked for a little foundation for ten years and ran it for five. At the end of that time I had come to believe I was very wise indeed. The reason, in retrospect, was simple. Applicants for foundation money rarely dispute the dispenser. In fact, they reinforce extravagantly any suspicion the dispenser may have that he is cleverer than other people. Applicants tend to treat a suggestion that it is time for lunch as a bold and original insight. In time the best balanced of us accept the idea that we are extraordinarily smart cookies.

The simple and obvious truth is that a foundation is nothing more nor less than a bank account. It is not necessarily or even probably smart money. It is rare to find exceptionally gifted people in the foundation business. I have been hanging around the back stairs of American philanthropy for more than twenty years. A tiny handful of foundation people are outstandingly creative and imaginative. Most are ordinary, and a considerable minority are fools.

Moreover, foundations tend to be schizophrenic. They are drawn to two widely contradictory views of their mission. One view is what is sometimes called the Embree thesis—the idea that foundations are the pure research department of the American polity, providing social risk capital, pushing forward the frontiers of understanding, cheerfully accepting the fact that on knowledge's frontier, failure is more common than success. This is really heady stuff and leads to grants for projects with titles like these: "The origin and significance of the decorative types of medieval tombstones in Bosnia and Herzegovina" and "The remains of rural chthonic traditions which existed in Europe during the Middle Ages."

The other view is somewhat overlapping and grows out of a mistaken assumption that a foundation's prerogatives are conferred, so to speak, by government. "All foundation monies are really part of the public monies," writes S. Dillon Ripley, secretary of the Smithsonian Institution. In other words, foundations exist at the pleasure of government, so they are morally subject and, increasingly, legally subject to the same kind of majoritarian review as the expenditures of the Department of Defense. Foundations, according to this view, live on subsidies, except that the postage is saved, and so they should operate within a definition of the public interest which is acceptable to

Congress. Now, this view is quite a different matter from the Embree thesis. The average Congressman's idea of a sensible benefaction is a grant to Boys Town.

So foundations try to satisfy both these perceptions of their role at once. The result is often silly. The foundation I worked for once made a considerable grant to the Airmail from God Mission, which dropped Protestant pamphlets from airplanes over Catholic provinces in Mexico.

Foundation officials make speeches about risk-taking, and make grants to the most prosaic and conventional causes. When the staff of the Peterson Commission asked these bold risk-takers how many of their grants were in fact even controversial, and the answers were compiled, it came out to one tenth of one percent. Foundations claim that 3 percent of their grants are "innovative," but when I look for examples of foundation-sponsored social innovation, I can find very little.

If you press foundation people for specific examples of foundation-financed innovation, they will usually give you two: the Rockefeller Foundation's conquest of hookworm in 1909, and the legendary Flexner report, published just after World War I, which recommended some changes in medical education. If foundations have an inherent capacity for social invention, they have certainly not exercised it with much success—at least, not lately.

Some foundation people confess the innovation theory is a pose. "We sometimes kid around about being on the cutting edge of social change," a Ford Foundation staff member told Taylor Branch. "What that means is funding something the government might pick up in two or three years."

The point is that both the conflicting perceptions of the

foundation's role are wrong. The Embree thesis may have been right for Embree, but as a generalization about the natural "role" of foundations, it is plausible nonsense. Leaving aside the fact that it is usually impossible to distinguish radical truth from lunacy before the fact, why should the heirs and cronies of some successful noodle manufacturer suddenly become the pioneers of change?

Foundations restrict themselves with superstitious rules. Like pampered teenagers, they know mainly what they won't do. Some won't give money for "bricks and mortar." Many won't give money for operating budgets. Most are aggressively fickle, saying they will only finance projects for a year or two. Thus is the social landscape littered with projects foundations started and refused to finish.

At a time when the nation desperately needs some diversity, foundation agendas reflect instead a dead and discouraging similarity.

Foundations should fire their experts and find out who they are. They should finance what they believe in. They should act on problems which they know firsthand or feel deeply about. (Ross Perot showed a fine quixotic flair for philanthropy when he tried to fly to Hanoi to negotiate the release of the prisoners of war.) The result would be a healthy "natural" diversity. Foundations are not common carriers. They need not be ashamed of their heritage. They need only to develop a solid sense of legitimacy and self-respect.

They should work out, methodically, a profile of their strengths, weaknesses and—most of all—their convictions. The foundation I most respect—the Stern Fund—is a committed foundation. It pursues convictions—many of which I happen not to share—with unusual determination and imagination.

A recent Stern Fund report lists, among others: a grant to help a neighborhood group in Illinois buy a bank; a grant to study whom the government is watching with what electronic devices; a grant to Stewardesses for Women's Rights to help build self-esteem among female flight attendants; a grant to pay for a skiing program for blind people; a grant to study radical alternatives to the American "system"; and a grant to search for ecologically sound ways to farm in cities—like backyard fish farms.

The Stern Fund adds to the texture of America. It enlarges the range of choice. It produces action and reaction. It is alive.

I don't know all the details of Henry Ford's own giving, but it would be interesting to compare the social results of his naïve, impulsive and sentimental philanthropy with the supersophisticated programs the Ford Foundation brews in its East Side ice palace. When World War I was gathering, the old man bought a ship, called it the "Peace Ship," filled it with American citizens and sailed it to the shores of Europe to talk things over. Sensing that mass production was changing the face of America, he put millions into building Greenfield Village. Two generations later, we are coming to realize the need to substitute personal for governmental diplomacy, and we are scrambling to rescue relics of the way of life progress has displaced.

Private philanthropy exists as an alternative not because private boards are inherently wiser and more sensible than Congress or a federal bureaucracy, but because they have a million more chances to be wise.

The organizations of what I call the independent sector (it has no generally accepted name) have also radically mistaken their identity. There are probably millions of them in America—no one knows for sure—ranging from Alcoholics Anonymous and the Association for the Study of Abortion to the Zen Institute of America and Zonta International, a fifty-year-old association of women in business. These organizations are imprisoned, their ambition limited, by a feeling that they are obsolete, that they were capable of large accomplishments when the world was younger and simpler. Now they suffer from self-induced senility.

As a group, they have an acute inferiority complex. I often quote a Columbia economist who once said, when questioned about the future of independent action, that perhaps such organizations could run dog cemeteries and bird sanctuaries but were no longer fit to take more serious responsibility.

Now, the fact is that no one knows for sure what the independent sector might accomplish if it recovered its confidence. I believe myself that its potential is vast. But it cannot now grow beyond its limited sense of its capacities— except accidentally.

For years its leadership has accepted the jobs that are best done on the cheap. For example, independent organizations are supposed to have a special facility for developing new social therapies which, once they are pre-tested, can be taken over by the government. But the independent sector should never, the superstition goes, presume to deliver in scale—it is not suited for that. It is supposed to function as an auditor of government—a passive role—or as an advocate of more government action.

So the independent sector tends to view itself as a comparatively slender national resource, inventive, but not reliable over the long pull, passive and mildly persuasive—the qualities of an aging, well-meaning, loquacious absent-minded professor.

I see no evidence that any of these self-perceptions are at all accurate. They certainly aren't drawn from any solid evidence. As government has taxed away the money which would otherwise nourish the independent sector and moved recklessly and impulsively into one field after another, it has left the independent sector less and less apparent work to do, and less and less money to spend.

But the fact is that the independent sector is so diverse, and growing more so every day—several thousand new block associations have been formed in New York City alone in the last few years—that any generalization about its capacities is probably wrong.

The independent sector is sometimes inventive, as when Jonas Salk found an effective polio vaccine. It is sometimes effective as an advocate of government action—hundreds of independent agencies lobby fervently for new government programs—although it is probably never as good at selling new government programs as is the government itself, the myth of government reluctance to expand notwithstanding. Independent organizations do often act as watchdogs over government programs—most large cities have privately financed governmental research agencies—but whether anybody can be effective in this role is an open question.

The independent sector is certainly not inconstant. Many of its agencies have been delivering services faithfully and consistently for decade after decade. Harvard was founded in 1638, Massachusetts General Hospital in 1811, the YMCA in 1851, the American Red Cross in 1861, the American Cancer Society in 1913.

There is evidence that when given the opportunity, the independent sector is better at the massive delivery of services than the government is—for example, the National Foundation's almost totally successful immunization programs against polio—though probably not so good as commercial organizations.

The independent sector seems to me to be absorbing change more quickly than government institutions but not as quickly as commercial organizations.

In short, the organizations of the independent sector have been trapped in a limiting self-perception. But they are beginning to reconsider their origins and possibilities.

Probably the American institution with the least accurate sense of identity is the federal government. It apparently believes it can do anything, and Congress seems to share that belief.

Peter Drucker has written that the federal government can do nothing but wage war and inflate the currency, and the military debacle in Southeast Asia suggests he was only half right.

I once suggested to the officials at the Department of Health, Education and Welfare that they devote some hours a week to reflecting on the basic nature of the department, asking themselves questions like these: What, exactly, is unique about federal action? What has HEW ever done that was effective? We decided, after a little thought, that the department's most far-reaching effects were unintended, as when its welfare program triggered the wholesale migration of poor Black people to the Northern cities.°

This suggests what reason reinforces—that government, which is distinguished from other institutions only by superior powers to tax and forbid, should use these powers principally to modify the atmosphere of incentives in which people and institutions function.

Thus there is already a perceptible tendency for government to act on the public business in new and promising ways—not by impulsively seizing every responsibility but by de-management, by devising methods which will release the imprisoned energies of nonfederal agencies.

That is the subject of the next chapter.

° Had the department tried to do this deliberately, with some federal "New Start" program, it would almost surely have failed.

# 14

# Taximeter Government

I like a mayor who doesn't meddle in city affairs.
—Joey Adams, at the Rainbow Grill

In Scottsdale, Arizona, the fire chief wears a business suit. He probably doesn't know it, but he is an accidental pioneer of a revolutionary change in the way legislative bodies all over the country are handling the public business. He works under contract to the Scottsdale City Council.

There is, of course, nothing new about governments contracting out some of the work they do. Most cities, in effect, "hire" a fire department to put out fires and a police department to keep the peace. What's different is that whereas most cities pay a fire department to repeat certain procedures that are assumed to be effective, Scottsdale pays a business to *get a result*. It doesn't say how. It is a small difference with enormous consequences.

This technique, which some people are beginning to call "performance contracting," is becoming the basis of the fastest-growing industry in America.

I haven't seen the Scottsdale contractor at work, but I understand he has introduced a generation of pent-up fire-fighting know-how in a handful of years. He found out, first of all, that fire trucks are the wrong color. Only black is less visible at night than fire-engine red. His trucks are a luminous yellow. He sensed, too, that fire trucks should be fast. The ones he designed are compact, maneuverable, fast-moving. He discovered that most houses burn down while firemen are looking for a hydrant, even though most fires can be extinguished with a portable supply of water. His trucks carry their own water, and in an amount carefully calculated to meet almost all his requirements. Fire engines, for some forgotten reason, are laden with expensive chrome. His are not. His employees wear white coveralls and yellow hard hats. They work at other things between fires, eliminating the deadening waste of waiting for fires to start. He gets much better results much cheaper. He is not a genius. It is only that Scottsdale has discovered how to manage without manipulation. He isn't hired simply to repeat traditional procedures. He gets his instructions in a way that welcomes and rewards workable innovation.

Performance contracting is emerging first where you might expect it last—in public education. A growing number of school districts are contracting with commercial educational organizations to run all or parts of their systems.

This is only the beginning. The boards of nearly sixty public and private hospitals have contracted their management to business firms in the last four years. Hospital Affiliates, the largest of the contract management companies, signed their first two contracts in 1971. By mid-1974 they were operating twenty-nine hospitals, sixteen of them governmental. Quality is maintained by twice-a-year tests of two hundred separate aspects of each hospital's performance. Every departing patient is surveyed, as is every doctor practicing in every hospital. Service is better, costs are often 25 percent less. Hospital Affiliates doesn't have to sell the service. They are getting ten to twenty inquiries a week from conventionally operated hospitals.

More and more parks, owned and "governed" by states or counties, are being operated by private companies. More than half the policemen in the country are on the payrolls of private protection companies, and firms like these are supplying contract police service to a growing list of towns and cities. Cities are hiring private companies to provide ambulance services, make building inspections, collect the garbage, and run the buses and subways.

Scanning the still spotty literature on the subject, I find that these private contractors provide better service for 30 to 40 percent less money. The possibilities are immense. Students of the trend predict that performance contracting of traditionally public functions may in time become the nation's largest industry.*

We can expect to see the use of the method in operating prisons, mental health facilities, parking lots and a hundred other government functions. But there is one essential precondition for the expansion of performance contracting. Government must learn how to order. It must learn to describe the results it wants *precisely*. But this, it seems to me, is what governments are for.

Another practical method of de-managing the public business with an abundance of possible applications is the

---

* The performance-contracting method is not magically immune to abuse. But, historically and logically, its abuses are much more readily perceived and corrected.

use of vouchers. Distributing vouchers is simply a way to get bread to people who can't afford it without bureaucratizing the bakeries, or to give poor children a chance to see wild animals without nationalizing the zoos.

Government issues a kind of scrip to people who need some service and presumably can't afford it—educational or legal services or practically anything that is individually consumed—redeemable by approved or licensed suppliers of the service. The use of vouchers is promising because the government does not say *how* the service shall be delivered. It simply creates a demand, and invites an open-ended response to meeting it. It limits government to the business of deciding who needs how much subsidy.

Some cautious experiments with vouchers are already under way. A year ago, Stacy Getman, along with four thousand other children in Alum Rock Union School District in California began the school year by handing her teacher an engraved green voucher. Such vouchers are redeemable only at the six public schools in the district, so the options open to the students are limited. But they are six times greater than they were before.

The experiment in California is very young, but already diverse approaches to teaching are beginning to bud. One school features computers and space technology. Another is stubbornly traditional. The experiment may not work, but it has a few more chances to work than the monolithic, managed system it replaced. The idea that education can be demanaged is perceived as revolutionary. Berkeley law professor John E. Coons says, "The whole notion that people might be able to make choices about their children's lives is . . . something that's never been tried before."

The performance principle is proving itself even in the

blindingly complex business of city planning. Ada Louise Huxtable, *The New York Times*' brilliant architectural critic, is, happily, hard to please. But she likes what is happening to Lower Manhattan. In a story headlined "Innovative Designs Are Beginning to Take Shape and Transform Lower Manhattan," she writes, "The new premise is that you attempt to control only the points where the public interest meets the private domain."

The city legislates certain fixed requirements: that builders respect traditional street patterns or provide waterfront promenades or include multilevel arcades. "But," writes Ms. Huxtable, "beyond those requirements, there are no holds on how a builder designs or builds. He is no longer subjected to costly, time-consuming reviews, political delays or bureaucratic caprice. . . . The instruments used at the interfaces between public areas and private development are called performance controls." So we can see the magic of demanagement solving a problem that has vexed the planners for years—the harmonization of an unmanageable diversity into a rational, workable overall result.

Even in the humble business of building codes, many communities are demanaging—adopting the performance principle by substituting new "performance" codes for the traditional "specifications" codes.

A specifications code tells you that you have to use specific materials, like copper pipe, and thus it repeals technological change. If better pipe is made, builders can't use it, unless the code is changed, in which case you are up against the copper-pipe manufacturers. Specifications codes immortalize procedures and thus politicize building.

A performance code, on the other hand, simply defines what has to be done. It says pipe must withstand so-and-so-much pressure and last so-and-so long. So builders can use new materials if they perform. A specifications code prohibits innovation; a performance code invites it. And responsibility flows to the manufacturers whose materials work best. Performance codes tend to depoliticize homebuilding. People spend their energy developing new ways to do things instead of defending the old ways.

In Washington still another approach to demanaging the public business is emerging. Congress is beginning to learn to write laws that direct and redirect the flow of responsibility to whatever agencies are best able to take it.

Most federal legislation simply activates or modifies federal programs. Such legislation is usually based on some superstition about the adequacy of nonfederal institutions. It works like this:

1. A problem or need is perceived or invented.
2. The inadequacy of the nonfederal response is asserted—rarely, if ever, demonstrated.
3. A federal program is activated.
4. The nonfederal response is driven out.

The nonfederal response becomes inadequate simply because the federal folklore defines it as inadequate.

But federal legislation can be written in a way that invites and encourages nonfederal organizations to respond. Such legislation needs, principally, to define "adequacy" with some precision—to set a standard of performance.

Model federal legislation of this new type would have these qualities:

1. It would define "adequacy" precisely.
2. It would provide "stand-by" authority to the federal authorities so that the government could act auto-

matically—without further legislation—if nonfederal institutions failed to meet the defined standard of adequacy.

3. It would provide for the automatic termination of federal activity if and when nonfederal institutions achieved or regained their ability to provide an "adequate" response.

This kind of legislation, rare in our history, has some dramatic advantages: it activates and accelerates nonfederal action; it leaves government free to govern, by giving maximum responsibility for *action* to nonfederal entities; it means that nonfederal institutions earn their right to responsibility with results instead of rhetoric.

I once helped write this kind of law for student loan programs. I had organized a nationwide, independent program to guarantee prime-rate bank loans to college students. The federal government, asserting that our response was inadequate, proposed a federal program. We had no doubt that federal programers could drive us out of business if they wanted to, but we believed we could do a better job for much less money.

Congress wrote a law which would let us prove it. The law defined adequacy with an almost absurd precision. If a student had to drive less than twenty-five miles to get his money from a participating bank, that was considered adequate. Twenty-five miles plus one inch was inadequate. If the bank would loan the student $1,000 a year, that was "adequate"; $999.99 was called "inadequate." The law said the federal government could not start a federal loan program in any state unless it could prove that our response didn't meet the agreed-to definition of adequacy. And, for a while, it worked. We struggled to keep our organization alive by being "adequate." Students were served "adequately." No tax money was spent. The federal bureaucracy watched our program with a fierce vigilance, impatient to prove our inadequacy so they could start their program.

This kind of "specified response" legislation was embodied, at least in spirit, in the law which set up the Product Safety Commission in 1973. It is supposed to work like this. The commission collects information to find out what consumer products are in fact causing injuries. Whenever the hazard suggests that a new or revised product standard is needed, the commission invites applications from private agencies or groups who may want to develop such a standard. The commission selects from the applicants the one it thinks is best qualified to develop the standard. The commission can develop the standard itself *only* if no qualified body applies for the task, if the standard is not produced within a specified time, or if the standard is considered "inadequate."

This method, if it is observed faithfully, will encourage a multiple response to standards development. But it also provides a backup if private groups fail to respond. Federal intervention becomes selective. The federal agency can act only when private groups fail. I can imagine dozens of applications of this method of demanaging the public business—in housing, health, employment, drug regulation and many more.

So there are signs that America is de-managing the public business.

Tenure is under attack. Doctors are defrocking colleagues who make people sicker. The idea of accountability is ascendant. Were this process to continue, the specific consequences are unknowable, but certain general results are predictable. There would be massive shifts in the distribution of responsibility among America's institutions.

The federal government would in general have much less responsibility; independent organizations would have much more. Private companies would deliver the mail and collect the garbage.

The federal government's social responsibility would become largely a stand-by responsibility—a series of commitments to act if and when nonfederal organizations failed to meet carefully defined standards of service.

Public service institutions—schools, hospitals, prisons and the like—would continue to be *governed* by official or semiofficial ruling bodies which would set performance standards, but they would, as a rule, be *operated* by nongovernmental organizations.

Government would sometimes subsidize consumers of certain services, but it would no longer subsidize the institutions providing service.

There would be a reexpansion of the prerogatives of private philanthropy. Most of the limits on the option to give money to independent agencies would be removed.

The federal government would in time move out of the regulatory field entirely, and be displaced by increasingly effective patterns of independent third party regulation.

There will be a dramatic increase in the private performance of traditionally public functions, possibly extending even to diplomacy.

The amount of energy and imagination applied to the public business would increase massively, as de-management released the imprisoned energies of our institutions.

But to call the experiments in de-management a trend

would be, as Dr. Johnson once said in another connection, a triumph of hope over experience. They prove only that we are failing to de-manage not because we don't know how, but for other reasons.

# Part VI

# What We
# Are Becoming

# 15

# The Process of Change

> . . . there are always islands of self-sufficient order—on farms and in castles, in homes, studies, and cloisters—where sensible people manage to live relatively lusty and decent lives, as moral as they must be, as free as they may be, and as masterly as they can be. If we only knew it, this elusive arrangement is happiness.
>
> —Erik H. Erikson

I was an NAM executive for three years.

After the first few weeks I was very uncomfortable there. Every day, I was instructed to do things I found unnatural and distasteful. I was afraid of my boss, a kindly, driven man with a forced smile who dealt with employees like a prosecuting attorney. He kept on the coffee table in his office a replica of a medieval mangler, which he would handle wistfully once in a while. I found the NAM a fear-ridden, stuffy place.

But I stayed there anyway, miserable and half afraid all the time. And the longer I stayed, the more my resentment toward my boss grew, until I could scarcely stand the sight of him. I made long detours to the toilet to avoid seeing him, shirked my duties most shamefully, and rode home at night grim and tense.

At last I quit. Months later I realized that my outrage toward my boss was misdirected. There are necessarily two parties to any authoritarian relationship—the one who manages and the one who permits himself to be managed. I had finally and half accidentally freed myself. And when I did, I became a part of a revolution.

When I first came to New York in the mid-sixties, I would sometimes go to uptown cocktail parties and listen to svelte young women in Pucci dresses talking feverishly about "the revolution." I was puzzled. I am from small-town Indiana and I tend to take things literally. To me "revolution" meant death and ripped flesh and agony, and I knew these bloodthirsty drawing-room Bolsheviks were afraid to ride the subway.

But then more recently I began to hear warmer, younger people talking softly and matter-of-factly about the revolution, and I began to take it more seriously. And I soon realized that they mean it metaphorically, as Episcopalians mean "the second coming."

This "revolution" is real, and it has enormous permanent power. Millions and millions of people are involved in it, and more are enlisting every day. And it is a revolution of an entirely different sort. It aims not for the substitution of one authority for another, but for the final transformation of authority. It is moving on many different fronts. Its weapons are self-discovery and self-expression. I don't believe it will ever be turned back.

The revolution is me, quitting NAM.

The revolution is a young radio actress who flatly refuses to read lines that demean women.

The revolution is an architect who quit designing airports and office buildings and began redesigning personal products—toothbrushes and eyeglasses—because he did not want to design beyond his own experience.

The revolution is a *Wall Street Journal* editorialist writing: "The job for America, in the end, may be to replace the idea of success with the idea of the soul."

The revolution is Andy Dodge in Topeka saying he will never go back to managed employment. It is Carl Tendler operating proudly on his own in Greenwich Village.

The revolution is five thousand new block associations formed in New York City in the last three years—people taking into their own hands the responsibility for the peace and care of their neighborhoods.

The revolution is disillusioned liberal activist Will D. Campbell conducting an eccentric redneck ministry in Tennessee. According to journalist Marshall Frady, he has "passionately repudiated all the familiar liberal engines for creating a just society—legislation, politics, programs. He insists that institutions . . . merely magnify the estrangements between people. The only hope for revolutionizing society does not lie in its institutions but in revolutionizing . . . the hearts of men."

The collective efforts of such people are, and probably always have been, the most powerful cause of change.

Management can survive only if people submit to it. And more and more people, as they develop a sharper sense of their full human potential, are saying in one way or another that they will *not* take their places in line anymore, that they will *not* be housebroken, that they will *not* be treated like furniture.

A new kind of society is displacing the old. Unofficially, outside the political process, America is de-managing itself.

And there are signs that we are outgrowing the illusion that new wizards in Washington will somehow set things right. A disaffection with politics is becoming epidemic. People are not voting. The press, predictably, called Nixon's victory over McGovern a "landslide." But their obsession with politics caused them to overlook the fact that it was the smallest vote since 1948. Forty-five percent of the people eligible to vote didn't vote at all. If you rearrange the returns to include this reality, the picture changes radically: McGovern 22 percent, Nixon 33 percent and 45 percent abstaining. The election was a landslide, all right, but it was—if anything—a landslide for political disaffection.

"More and more voters," wrote R. W. Apple in *The New York Times* a few days before the 1974 congressional elections, "appear to have concluded that nothing they can do with their ballots can change things. . . . Americans seem to care deeply about a large number of issues, while at the same time feeling impotent to effect any real solutions."

"We're in danger of looking on politics as a spectator sport," said pollster Patrick Caddell. "It doesn't do any more for your life than pro football. You're a little unhappy when the home team loses, but it's not serious business."

The pollsters' predictions were right. Last year only 38 percent of the eligible voters went to the polls, down 17 percent from 1972—the lowest vote in modern history.

"This isn't apathy or laziness," Caddell said, "it is a rational decision not to participate."

At the mention of government, writes Purdue professor Michael O'Neill, "[students'] minds move *en masse* out the window."

There are other signs. Civil disobedience of one sort or another has become nearly universal. Tax revolt, unthinkable a few years ago, is now at least a discussable possibility. Sensible people are leaving political life, not, as they have often done before, because it is inherently dirty—which it is and always will be—but because of a deeper kind of disillusion.

Politics can now attract only the most limited of men. People who want power—and get it—are unfit to govern. Dr. Guy Pauker of the Rand Corporation says, "The concept and profession of politics has been discredited." And Theodore Hesburgh, president of Notre Dame, writes in *Newsweek*, "It is not that America lacks leaders—rather that most of them are avoiding Washington like the plague."

Politics is becoming obsolete. Its swollen importance in the public consciousness is based on the myth of the effectiveness of power. It is certainly true that people of all sorts are just now seeking political power more feverishly than ever. But I suspect this may be due to a subliminal suspicion that political power may soon have little value.

There are subtler signs. Legislatures are still grinding out alchemistic programs, passing laws and raising taxes. The courts, as if to fill the vacuum, are legislating—redefining the rights of people and institutions in ways that have had effects far beyond anything the Congress has done in a generation. Millions of young people are leaving the political parties. In Gallup's most recent poll of party preferences, most students expressed none. A historic 40 percent of the whole population are not members of any party, but "independent." If it is legitimate to attribute elaborate motives to the people who vote—as all the pundits do—it is fair to speculate about the intentions of the people who don't—who are kicking the political habit.

I believe there is building in America a new silent

plurality—a growing group who believe that our complaints are organic and beyond the reach of politics as we now practice it. More and more of us are sensing that our country is in a kind of trouble that cannot be cured by conventional political action, but by its unfamiliar opposite —by de-politicizing, or de-managing, a society that has outgrown its present structures and is not working. The silent plurality may be longing to fix America without politics and wondering where to begin.

The most powerful potential political force in America is, at the moment, dormant. People everywhere are straining toward what it is proper and possible for them to be, but unmanaged America is still unsure of its strength and legitimacy.

But beyond the present process of consciousness raising—which is inner-directed and passive—may be a new kind of activism. More people may, as Blacks and women have done, begin to insist that their rights be more precisely defined and more carefully observed.

The Bill of Rights has lost most of its meaning. There is no effective limit on government's power to tax and command, to destroy the value of our money, to invade our privacy, to wage war and to strap us into our motorcars. But the people can, when they want to, redefine their rights and force the front office to accept whatever definitions they devise.

The managers will never de-manage society, but maybe the people will.

# Afterword

Now that it is finished, I find this book is very largely a rearrangement of ideas I have borrowed from other people.

She doesn't know it, but Rose Friedman put the theme of it in my head in a passing line she wrote in an essay about poverty in 1965.

A very central idea—that businessmen insist on acting in an unmanaged atmosphere while they overmanage the people who work for them—belongs to Bennett Kline.

I learned such economics as I know at the feet of Ludwig von Mises, whose knowledge of the subject was so complete that he even knew its limitations.

I have drawn most extravagantly on the work of F. A. Hayek, who is, I believe, by any honest measure, the most original and important social theorist of the century. One chapter of this book is simply a pop version of his splendid essay *The Use of Knowledge in Society.*

In the parts on public policy, I have used ideas that were original with Milton Friedman, and with Roger Freeman.

Carle Zimmerman first showed me that sociology need not be trivial.

Jane Jacobs' work was indispensable.

Then there are more personal debts: to Martha Stuart who led me into the world outside the front office which I would never have found without her—this is her book; to Suzie who fought her way to freedom all by herself and then shared what she found there with me; to Peter who taught me about thinking when he was six and I was thirty-seven; to Jenny whose vision of the future is so large and bright; and to George Harris, who again and again gently encouraged me to keep going.

And I am thankful to the other people who have listened to me and helped me in various ways: Betty Friedan, Amitai Etzioni, Willy Watman, Alfred de Grazia, Gershon Kekst, Donna Welensky, Edna Cash, Jason Epstein, Elizabeth Fonseca.

I want to mention some scholars and writers whose work has particularly helped me and which seems to me to be of special importance: Peter Drucker, Paul Goodman, Ivan Illich, Abraham Maslow, Erich Fromm, Irving Kristol, Robert Coles, Charles Reich, Studs Terkel, Helmut Schoeck.

I am grateful to the Hoover Institution and its director, Glenn Campbell, who gave me a grant to write the book and then patiently let me work without management.

Finally, I want to mention a man whose name I never knew who gave me the book's hidden text. One day in South Bend, I hailed a cab for the airport, and the driver was a young man, in his early twenties. He was probably what we have been taught to call "retarded," but in his case it came out as a sweet and engaging simplicity. We talked about South Bend and the world outside that he hardly knew, and as we talked the radio blared the harsh, harried voice of his company's dispatcher. We stopped talking for a while to listen, and then my driver sighed and said, "I'd hate to have that dispatcher's job." (He pronounced it DISS-pacher.) "It's all I can do to dispatch myself."

R.C.

New York
December, 1974

RICHARD CORNUELLE was an executive vice-president of the National Association of Manufacturers from 1966 to 1969, and is the author of *Reclaiming the American Dream*. He lives in New York City.